Bite-size activities for music teaching at K...

Sound bites

Richard Frostick and Lin Marsh

www.fabermusic.com/schoolsmusic

CD recorded in Rectory Studio, High Wycombe, February 2004.
Voices: Lin Marsh and Richard Frostick
Piano: John Lenehan
Engineered by John Lenehan
Produced by Leigh Rumsey
℗ 2004 Faber Music Ltd   © 2004 Faber Music Ltd

© 2004 by Faber Music Ltd
First published in 2004 by Faber Music Ltd
3 Queen Square London WC1N 3AU
Design by Susan Clarke
Music processed by Jackie Leigh
Printed in England by Caligraving Ltd
All rights reserved

ISBN 0-571-52555-5

FABER *ff* MUSIC

Introduction

This is a book of songs and ideas for all primary classroom teachers. We hope that both non-specialist and specialist music teachers will find the activities accessible, jargon-free and stimulating.

The topics are based on everyday happenings that take place in a thousand school classrooms across the school year. The activities can be used to provide a musical dimension to these events as they occur: a fire drill can lead to *Sirens and bells*, or a forthcoming school trip to *Visiting museums and galleries*. Many of the topics could form the basis for an entire unit of work.

Musical skills thrive when practised little and often. An ideal curriculum will combine frequent, short bursts of activity with more extended sessions. Many of the activities here will fit neatly into five and ten minute slots as they stand, or can be developed and combined to provide material for longer bursts. Precisely how you incorporate them into your work is left to your professional discretion. All the materials are in line with National Curriculum guidelines and will complement any scheme of work. For a list of contents, see page 48.

The songs in this book have all been specially written by Lin Marsh. A CD of accompaniments is included. However, you may prefer to download the piano accompaniments from **www.fabermusic.com/schoolsmusic**

> To give you guidance as to age-appropriateness, you will find icons by each activity; a key to these icons can be found below:
>
> ◉ = Years 1 and 2
>
> ✽ = Years 3 and 4
>
> ✪ = Years 5 and 6

As well as following this guidance we hope that you will use the book as a broader resource. Much of the fun in teaching lies in spotting a good idea, and from it, developing activities that will work for *your* class. As you roam through the book, take any activity – maybe one that at first glance looks too 'young' or 'old' for your pupils – and challenge yourself to re-present it in a format that would be appropriate to their ages and abilities.

Richard Frostick

Tips on singing

- Talk to the children about where their 'tank of fuel' for singing is! Explain that air is the fuel to power their voices and so their tanks (diaphragms) need to be wide and backs straight, with no slumping. This is particularly important if they are sitting on the floor.
- Wake up lips and tongues by chewing imaginary gum with big, wide, open mouths.
- Try voicing a gentle siren up and down the voice using the sound 'ng'. Keep it quiet and feel the muscles warming up as the voice travels through the different pitches.
- Explore various expressions to wake up the facial muscles. Try sad, angry, surprised, bored … Notice how the eyebrows in particular have a lot of work to do!

Teaching the songs using the CD

- Listen to the whole song and discuss its style and meaning; is it funny, serious, sad?
- Listen again and notice what in particular makes it special; which words seem important?
- How loud or quiet is it? What speed is it? Are there any very long or short notes?
- Listen to just the first line, then sing it with the CD.
- Listen to lines 1 and 2 and then copy.
- Keep on building a line at a time until you have learnt the whole verse or chorus.
- Try this part of the song with the accompaniment-only track.
- Listen to the complete track occasionally, to check that the notes are correct and the words are as clear as possible.
- Always check the children are singing with good posture, appropriate expression and clear diction – ensure they are using their singing voices, rather than shouting.

Rounds

There are two rounds (or 'canons') in this book: 'I can hear a bee!' and 'Late again'. On the CD, you will find a demonstration track with the round sung straight through rather than a piano accompaniment, as there are so many different ways of beginning and ending. Use this track to help teach the round to your pupils, or as a way of learning the round yourself.

When performing the round, try dividing the class into groups, allocating each a line to sing over and over. Alternatively, learn the complete round and bring in one group after another, four bars apart. As for endings: you could all finish together with a hand signal, or fade out one by one – see which works best with your pupils.

Lin Marsh

Taking the register

Rhythm register

Give the children a minute to look around and see who's present, then clap a steady pulse with them: 1 2 3 4. When this is secure, clap 1 2 and then the rhythm 'Manchester United' in place of 3 and 4 (**CD track 1**). In order to avoid a football riot, don't tell them the words, just clap them!

Pulse:	1	2	3	4
Class	1	2	Manchester	U-nited

Then call each pupil's name over the 1 2, alternating with you and the whole class clapping the 'Manchester United' rhythm. You must fit the pupil's name over 2 beats (**CD track 2**).

Pulse:	1	2	3	4
Class	1	2	Manchester	U-nited
Teacher:	Lin	Marsh	Manchester	U-nited

When you come to the name of a pupil who is absent, the class must not clap the 'Manchester United' rhythm. If anyone does they're out! If there is a gap for an absent pupil, pause, count to 4, and start again with the next pupil.

Dynamic register

In the following three activities ask the children to answer their names at the same level of volume that you have used.

1 Speak the first name loudly, the second quietly, third loudly, fourth quietly and so on – alternating loud and quiet. Can all the 'loud' pupils put their hands up? The 'quiet' ones? Link this with maths and odd/even numbers.

2 Repeat activity 1, but make the patterns increasingly complicated. Try two names loud and one soft, two loud, one soft. Ask the children to identify the pattern when you've finished.

3 Start reading the register in a whisper. As you go down the list gradually increase the volume (*crescendo*) until, by the seventh or eighth name, you are at your loudest. Then gradually get quieter (*diminuendo*) until by the fourteenth or fifteenth you are back at a whisper. Repeat the cycle up to the last name. Try not to let the pitch of your voice get higher and lower, just vary the volume. Ask the children to explain what you were doing. Which two names were the loudest? Which three names were the quietest? Could they draw what you did?

Pitch register

1 If you're a fairly confident singer, call out each name to a short melody; the whole class must respond by singing it back. Like 'Rhythm register', if someone's absent the class must not sing back.

2 Try activities 1 and 2 from 'Dynamic register' but vary the pitch of your voice instead; the first name in a high voice, the second in a low one etc. The children's responses should copy your pitch.

Speedometer!

When you're feeling particularly uninhibited, read the register as quickly as you possibly can. Then read it in slow motion. Or start slowly and put your foot on the accelerator …

Structure

Read the first half of the names quietly and the second loudly. If A is the first half and B the second, the whole structure could be described as A B. In music when you have one melody followed by a new one we describe the whole piece as 'binary' (two sections – A B). If you repeat the first section at the end it becomes 'ternary' (three sections – A B A). Ask the children how you could read the register in ternary form. (See also 'Patterns and structures' in *Visiting museums and galleries*, page 44.)

Vocal registers

Explain that the word 'register' has other meanings. The singing voice has different registers; low, middle and high. Play the children examples of singers with phenomenal ranges, for example: Natalie Dessay singing 'Bell Song' from *Lakme*, Léo Delibes; Cleo Laine singing 'Ridin' high' from *Ridin' high* (*The British Sessions 1960–1971*); Tuvan throat singers.

Wet play

Wet play today!

In a resigned manner!

It's wet out-side, we can't go out to play, it's wet out-side, we're stuck in here all day. The win-dows are all steam-y, the class-room's such a mess, and when the rain will stop, well we real-ly just can't guess. Our tea-chers all are suf-fer-ing from "Rain-y wea-ther stress" be-cause it's wet play to-day!

1. The rain keeps fal-ling down the win-dow pane, the sun has ne-ver shown its face, We'd love to play a game of foot-ball but there's wa-ter all a-round the place! It's

2. We're tired of sit-ting play-ing qui-et games, we're feel-ing bored as bored can be, We'd love to splash in all the pud-dles but our teach-er sim-ply won't a-gree! It's

CODA
wet play to-day!

'We'd love to splash in all the puddles'

Words about water are some of the most expressive in the language. Brain storm 'water words' on the board; just ask the children to think of as many as they can: splash, drip, wash, trickle, gush, drop, gurgle, squelch, spray, shower, splat. Let them make some up: 'squeege', 'splosh', 'squidge' etc.

When you have a fair selection, ask five children to form a line facing the class. Each child must choose one water word. Think of them as five notes on a weird instrument (a mermaid's piano, or a shark's keyboard), but instead of a note you get a water word. Go up and down the line pointing to individuals, trying two notes together, one twice as fast as the other – just like playing a keyboard. Then choose a pupil to splash around on the human keyboard. Make the keyboard longer. Extend the activity by having several 'keyboards' and 'players' going at once!

Ask them why they think so many water words have 's' and 'sh' sounds. Make the point by chanting 'Splash in puddles' a few times – the words sound like the activities they are describing.

Pools of sound

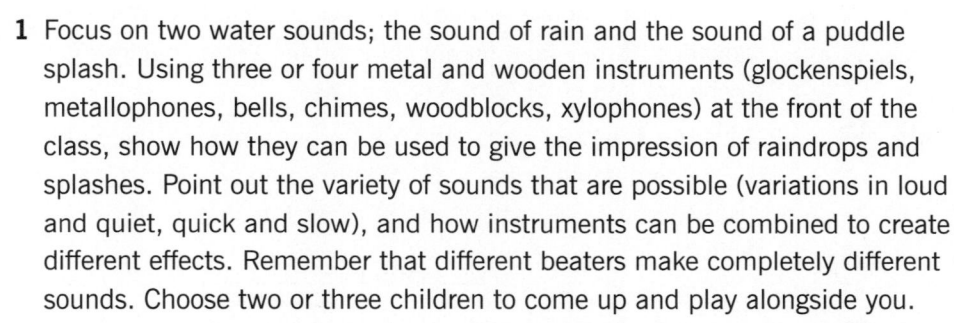

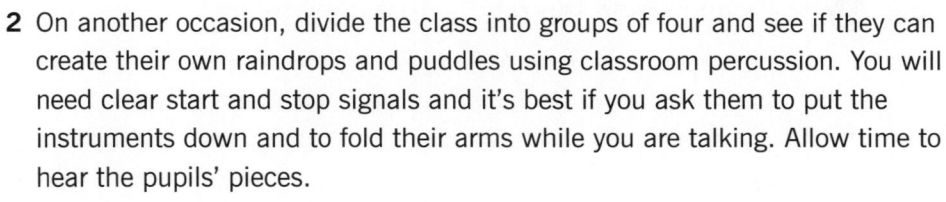

1 Focus on two water sounds; the sound of rain and the sound of a puddle splash. Using three or four metal and wooden instruments (glockenspiels, metallophones, bells, chimes, woodblocks, xylophones) at the front of the class, show how they can be used to give the impression of raindrops and splashes. Point out the variety of sounds that are possible (variations in loud and quiet, quick and slow), and how instruments can be combined to create different effects. Remember that different beaters make completely different sounds. Choose two or three children to come up and play alongside you.

2 On another occasion, divide the class into groups of four and see if they can create their own raindrops and puddles using classroom percussion. You will need clear start and stop signals and it's best if you ask them to put the instruments down and to fold their arms while you are talking. Allow time to hear the pupils' pieces.

3 Arrange the groups in a circle. Stand in the middle and show them that when you point directly at a group, the group must play. When you point to another, the first one must stop and the new one must play. See if you can get the effect of a 'wet playground', dodging from puddle to puddle in the rain. Ask a child to stand in the middle and conduct the sounds.

I'm board!

Every classroom has a dusty cupboard with some elderly board games. Draughts, chess, snakes and ladders – they're all there, and out they come at the first sign of wet play.

1 Make up a board game using sound. Try the idea on the following page:

Board squares (start → end):

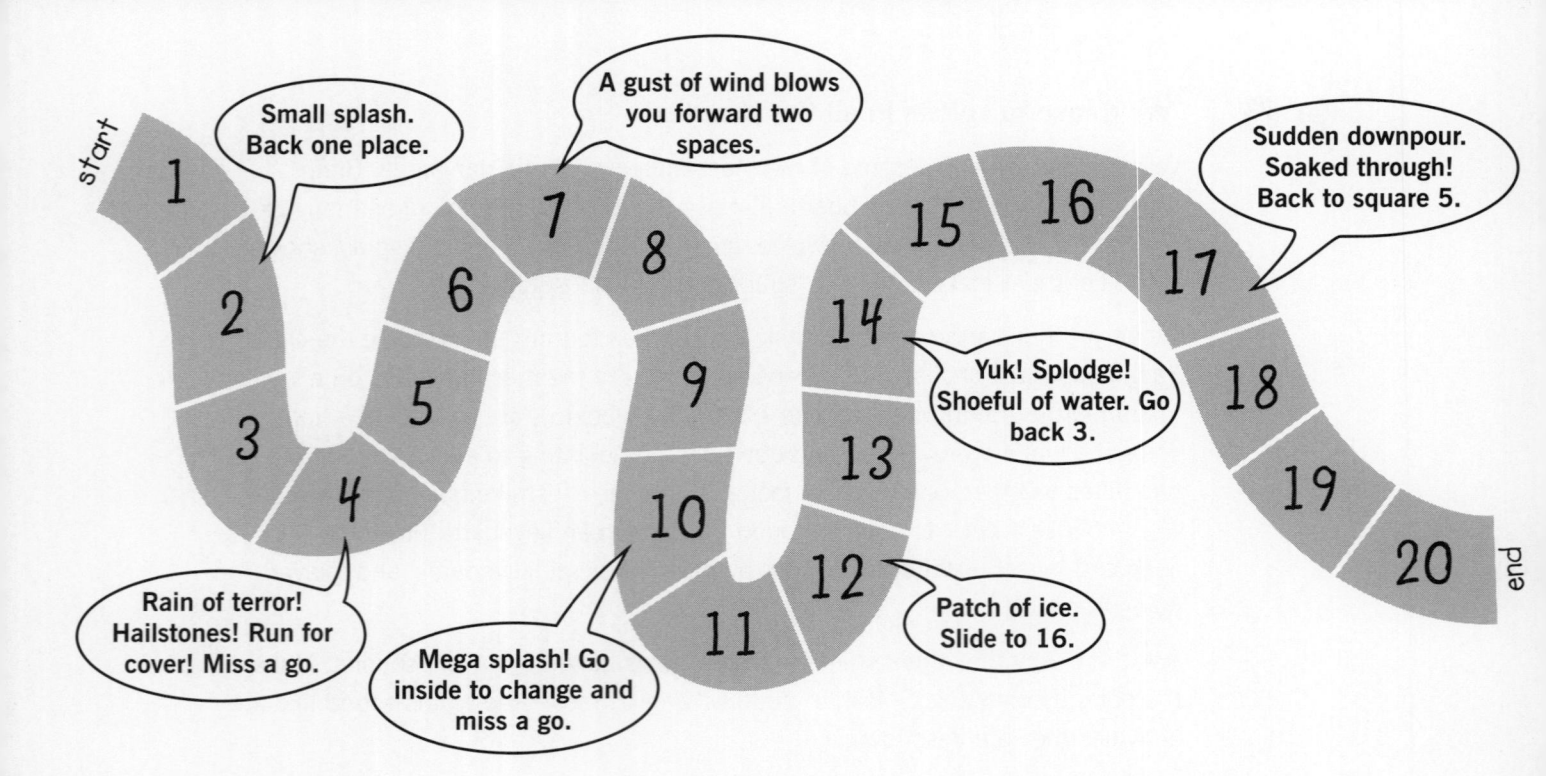

- start
- 1
- 2 — Small splash. Back one place.
- 3
- 4 — Rain of terror! Hailstones! Run for cover! Miss a go.
- 5
- 6
- 7 — A gust of wind blows you forward two spaces.
- 8
- 9
- 10 — Mega splash! Go inside to change and miss a go.
- 11
- 12 — Patch of ice. Slide to 16.
- 13
- 14 — Yuk! Splodge! Shoeful of water. Go back 3.
- 15
- 16
- 17 — Sudden downpour. Soaked through! Back to square 5.
- 18
- 19
- 20
- end

Have an orchestra of four or five children on classroom percussion to create the sounds. Choose a child to play the game; they throw the dice and advance. If they land on a sound square, the orchestra must play. Change the orchestra and child for the next game.

2 Give out sheets of paper and felt-tip pens and ask the children to devise their own board game in pairs. Give them some dice and get them to try it out, using a couple of instruments to make the sounds. A perfect wet-play activity!

'I can't stand the rain 'gainst my window'

Remember that one?! Making plants grow and stopping children play aren't the only things that rain can do – it also makes songs grow! Here are a few: 'Laughter in the rain', Neil Sedaka; 'The rhythm of the falling rain', The Cascades; 'Rainy night in Georgia', Brook Benton; 'Singin' in the rain', Gene Kelly; 'Raindrops keep fallin' on my head', Burt Bacharach; 'Here comes the rain again', Eurythmics; 'Fire and rain', James Taylor; 'It might as well rain until September', Carole King; there are dozens.

Find a recording of your favourite rain song and play it to the children. See if you can get them to identify any 'rain-like' features in the music. For example, in 'I can't stand the rain', there's a catchy rain motif just before the singing starts, and 'It might as well rain until September' ends with a rain motif gradually dripping to a stop.

Gardens in the rain

In other styles of music there are some wonderful examples of water painting in sound. 'Jardins sous la pluie' from *Estampes* by Claude Debussy is a spectacular piano piece where you can almost smell the dripping foliage. Play the children a recording of it and ask for their impressions.

Teeth

Please don't take a photograph!

Lively

1. I used to have a lovely smile, my teeth were neat and bright, just like a row of pearls they were, a really stunning sight. But one fell out at suppertime and left me with a space, it's hard to eat and hard to speak with gaps all round the place. So please don't take a photograph or make me smile or make me laugh, please don't give me apples 'cos I just can't bite! Listen very carefully for speaking is quite hard you see: put away your cam-'ra 'cos I'm not a pretty sight!

2. At first you feel a wobble then a tooth begins to creak, it wriggles back and forwards for the best part of a week. Then suddenly your tongue can feel a place that's new and weird: another tooth has fallen out, another gap's appeared.

Mind the gap!

Take a classroom metallophone or xylophone that has straightforward letter names on it (i.e. no sharps or flats). Write CDEFGABC on the board. Play this to the class several times. If possible gather the class around you so that the children can see you tap the scale as well as hear it. Then put a box or other obstruction between the pupils and the instrument. Play the eight notes again. Tell them that you are going to miss one out. To begin with make a slight pause over the missed note to help them identify it. Once they've got the hang of it, play without a break.

Draw a row of eight front teeth with a letter name on each. Which tooth has dropped out? Invite a pupil to take your role and play a scale with a missing note.

False tooth

Number the teeth as well as letter them. As a variation of 'Mind the gap!', deliberately play one wrong note, then carry on. Which number is the false tooth? Make the false tooth wildly obvious to begin with; with each repetition, make it increasingly subtle.

Filling!

Practise clapping a steady pulse of **1** 2 3 4 **1** 2 3 4 **1** 2 3 4. Put an extra 'bite' on each '1'. Explain that you want to get the effect of rows and rows of perfect, even white teeth – with one particularly shiny one every four!

Choose two or three of the steadiest clappers and ask them to continue clapping the pulse on their own. While they do this, lead the rest of the children in the following routine:

Pulse:	1	2	3	4	1	2	3	4
Teacher:	Clap	clap	knees	knees	1	2	3	4

Then lead all the pupils in 'Clap, clap, knees, knees, 1, 2, 3, 4', clapping, tapping the knees and taking the hands apart firmly on the 1 2 3 4. The effect will create a four-beat 'cavity' between each 'Clap, clap, knees, knees' (**CD track 7**).

Choose four pupils and give them each a tambourine, tambour, wood block or hand drum. Start a steady routine of 'Clap, clap, knees, knees, 1, 2, 3, 4' with the class. On each empty '1, 2, 3, 4' each of the four instrumentalists must fill the cavity with a sound or rhythm of their own. Each time you try this activity give the instruments to a different four pupils. Try to keep the pulse steady, even if some of the instrumental 'fillings' are a little eccentric to begin with!

Drop out!

Remember the popular party game 'Kim's game'? Play the class a range of percussion instruments – tambourine, bells, wood block, drum, maraca, guiro – and familiarise the pupils with their sound. Then play them in a different order out of sight; behind a bookcase or partition. See who can identify each one. The next time try two, one after the other. Which ones were they? Build up to three and then four. Who can name all four in the correct order? Then try it the other way round. Play a series of four instruments and then play it again, missing one out. Which one was missing?

Tooth music

Tap a simple tune on your front teeth! Allow the children to do the same – on their own teeth! If you can get hold of a microphone and portable amplifier, even better. What causes the notes to rise and fall? Guide them to make the link between the shape of the mouth and the tune. Explain that most wind instruments use this principle.

New growth

Talk about the growth of a new tooth. You can't see it actually moving, but each day you can see that it's grown a little. Who can make a sound grow very, very slowly? Take a tambourine and tap it very gently with one finger, moving gradually to the whole hand and increasing the volume. Invite a child to try this. Introduce the Italian term *crescendo* (gradually getting louder).

Tooth Fairy

Talk to very young children about the Tooth Fairy. What does she look like? What does she do with all those teeth? Does she sell them so that she can give you money? Use glockenspiels, bells and triangles to create Tooth Fairy music – it would have to be quiet, so as not to wake up the children. Who can move very lightly and quietly? Play them the 'Dance of the Sugar Plum Fairy' from *The Nutcracker* by Pyotr Ilyich Tchaikovsky.

Brush up your rhythm

Chant 'Brush, brush, brush, brush' steadily with the children. When this is established, chant 'Brushing, brushing, brushing, brushing' – one 'brushing' for each 'brush'. Divide the class in two; one half chants 'brush', the other 'brushing'. The dentist has told you that you are brushing too vigorously. How quietly can you go? Don't get slower!

Square roots!

During your numeracy hour sing some famous 'decreasing number' songs such as 'Three little monkeys' or 'Ten green bottles'. Can you change the words of 'Ten green bottles'?

> 'There were ten white gnashers, shining in a row;
> Ten white gnashers, shining in a row;
> And if one white gnasher, should accidentally go,
> There'd be nine white gnashers, shining in a row ...'

Sirens and bells

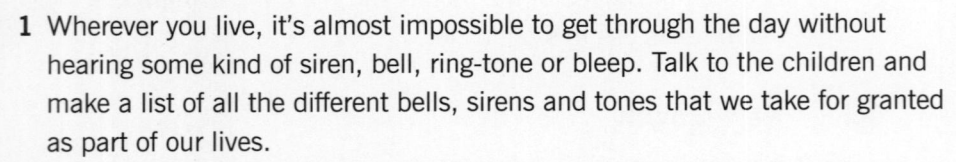

The bells, the bells

1 Wherever you live, it's almost impossible to get through the day without hearing some kind of siren, bell, ring-tone or bleep. Talk to the children and make a list of all the different bells, sirens and tones that we take for granted as part of our lives.

2 Prepare a tape of some well-known bells, tones and bleeps. Include your front door bell, telephone, cooker, alarm clock, car alarm, digital watch and school bell. Can they identify which is which?

Oranges and lemons

Sing the song 'Oranges and lemons' and play the game. Tell the class about the different churches and point out that the tune is derived from the sound of church bells. Play the beginning of the tune on a glockenspiel.

The history of nursery rhymes is always fascinating. Ask some older pupils to research 'Oranges and lemons' – it has particularly interesting origins.

You can ring my bell!

1 Ask the pupils to work in pairs, experimenting with their voices and mouths to create as many different bells, sirens and tones as they can. Start them off with a few yourself – try a fire-engine or digital watch alarm. Give the class three or four minutes and then hear some back. You'll be astonished at the range of sounds they'll produce.

2 Take four or five of the most striking sounds from activity 1. It would be fun to find out what they would sound like in various combinations. Sit the group of pupils in a line and invite one child to bring the sounds in and out at will. Use a drumstick – one (gentle!) tap on the shoulder means start, two taps means stop – or gestures and eye-contact.

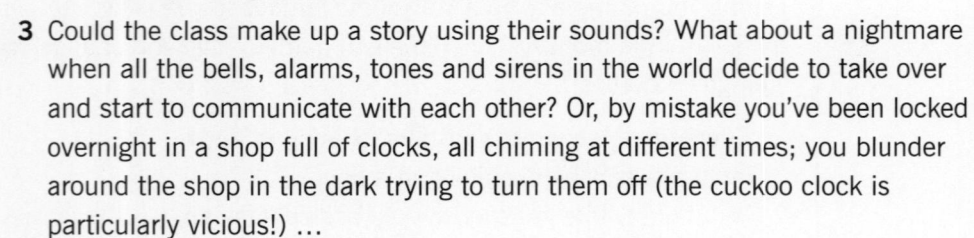

3 Could the class make up a story using their sounds? What about a nightmare when all the bells, alarms, tones and sirens in the world decide to take over and start to communicate with each other? Or, by mistake you've been locked overnight in a shop full of clocks, all chiming at different times; you blunder around the shop in the dark trying to turn them off (the cuckoo clock is particularly vicious!) ...

Mobile melodies

If you can sing it you can ring it! It's now possible to have your favourite melody as your mobile ring tone. Talk to the children about their (or their family's) mobiles and what music they use for the ring.

1 Find five or six distinctive ring-tone melodies on your own or a colleague's mobile phone. Play them to the children (if necessary, tape them first) and tell them what the music is. Find recordings of the original pieces and play them to the children. Use this as a starting point for exploring other music by these composers, or for telling them about their lives and times. There is

enough material here for a number of five-minute slots. Can they sing any of the themes? Can they clap the rhythms?

2 What melodies would the children most like to have as their own personal ring-tones? Do all tunes work, or do they need to have certain characteristics? Which melodies do they think various celebrities have as their personal ring-tones? What would a famous footballer have? The Queen? How many of the children can sing their suggestions?

Appeal of bells

Many religions use bells in their ceremonies and services. Christian religions use church bells to call the community to prayer and the art of bell ringing (campanology) is an ancient one.

1 Take some metal tuned classroom percussion instruments; glockenspiels and metallophones (without the sharps and flats) would be ideal. Show the children how striking the notes (lifting the beater clear of the note afterwards) can produce a delightful 'bell-like' sound. Experiment with beaters until you get the sound you want. Find the highest C and play, descending: C B A G F E D C. Immediately you will get the effect of church bells. You will discover that this is not as easy as it looks! The trick is to keep your eye on the notes. Try several children playing their peals of bells at once. Can anyone work out what Big Ben plays?

2 Many schools still have chime bars gathering dust in their cupboards. When they are played properly and used well, they can be useful and pleasant classroom instruments. If you have at least one set of C D E F G A B C you can try the activity above with one child to each note. Try to get the series as even as possible. Establish a pulse by tapping four beats steadily before you start. Ask a child to point to each player in turn, in time with your beat.

3 In bell-ringing, patterns are formed by changing the order of the notes. Choose a leader to point to the players, but this time not in strict descending order – ask them to experiment.

The magic of bells

1 Go through the school's instrument store and find as many different kinds of bells as you can. Add some triangles and some metal tuned instruments. Choose a group of 5 or 6 pupils and give them each a bell or other metal instrument. Experiment with the different sounds that can be created, both individually and in combination. Pay particular attention to the magic of quiet bells. What do they sound like?

2 There are many pieces of music that are memorable for their use of bells. Listen to the following; your children will be captivated: *Tubular Bells*, Mike Oldfield; *1812 Overture*, Pyotr Ilyich Tchaikovsky; 'Troika' from *Lieutenant Kije*, Sergei Prokofiev.

Tinkerbell

Read an extract from *Peter Pan* or show a clip from the Disney film involving Tinkerbell. Which instruments would best represent Tinkerbell? What would Tinkerbell's family sound like? Try out some possibilities.

Harvest festival

8/9 *What shall we bring for the Harvest festival?*

What shall we bring for the Har-vest fes-ti-val?
Who has a gift to-day? Love-ly things for the Har-vest fes-ti-val
What shall we bring to-day? We brought a tin of baked beans,
that's what we brought to-day! What shall we bring for the Har-vest fes-ti-val?
Who has a gift to-day? Love-ly things for the Har-vest fes-ti-val
What shall we bring to-day? We brought a tin of baked beans,

Repeat as necessary

2. loaf of bread* that's what we brought to-day!
3. pac-ket of bis-cuits
4. fruit cake
5. rice pudding
6. strawberry jam
7. salt and pepper
8. basket of apples

* Add an item to the song each time, counting upwards.

Rhythmic offerings

1 After singing 'What shall we bring for the Harvest festival?', practise clapping the food items over a repeated four-beat pulse. Clap 'tin of baked beans' as you say it and ask the children to copy. Then try all the items in the song; loaf of bread, packet of biscuits, fruit cake, rice pudding, strawberry jam, salt and pepper and basket of apples (**CD track 10**). Make sure that each item takes up four beats, even if there is a silent beat at the end:

1	2	3	4
Tin of	baked	beans	(rest)

Then try clapping the rhythms without the words.

2 Clap the rhythm of each food item and ask the children to guess what the food is.

3 Write the names of the food items from the song on the board. Invite a pupil to clap two rhythms one after the other, without missing a beat. The others must identify the food. Can they identify three in a row, or even four?

Harvest work songs

1 It isn't only food that is gathered in during harvest. Tell the pupils about cotton and where it grows. Then sing 'Pick a bale o' cotton' (**CD track 11**).

> 'Jump down, turn around, pick a bale o' cotton,
> Jump down, turn around, pick a bale a day.
> Jump down, turn around, pick a bale o' cotton,
> Jump down, turn around, pick a bale a day.
>
> Oh Lordy, pick a bale o' cotton,
> Oh Lordy, pick a bale a day.
> Oh Lordy, pick a bale o' cotton,
> Oh Lordy, pick a bale a day'.

Who could make up a dance to go with this?

2 Think of some British crops. Mime the action of picking something from trees. What are you picking – apples, pears, plums? Make the action rhythmic and ask the children to clap a pulse as you mime. Can you put some words to a tune that you know? Try:

> 'Pick an apple from the tree,
> From the tree, from the tree,
> Pick an apple from the tree,
> Fill that basket.'

… to the tune of 'London Bridge is falling down'. You now have your own harvest work song! Perform it with the class, with actions.

'Old Joe has gone fishing'

Listen to this wonderful chorus from the opera *Peter Grimes* by Benjamin Britten. It's one of the most challenging pieces to perform, although it is actually a round. See if anyone can spot this.

'Dance to your daddy' (CD track 12)

'Dance to your Daddy
My little babby,
Dance to your Daddy
My little lamb.
You shall have a fishy
In a little dishy,
You shall have a fishy
When the boat comes in.'

Practise clapping **1** 2 3 **1** 2 3 **1** 2 3 **1** 2 3 with an accent on the '1'. Who can dance to this?

Telling a story

✯ Words and music

1. Select five or six different classroom percussion instruments – a tambourine, woodblock, drum, bells, maracas and guiro would be ideal. Take one instrument and show the children the variety of sounds that are possible. Demonstrate how using different parts of the hands and fingers can change the sound (e.g. fingertips and fingernails, cupped hand and flat hand) and how different parts of the same instrument can sound different. Focus particularly on quieter sounds. Distribute instruments to the whole class and encourage a general exploration. Who has a particularly interesting technique or sound?

2. Write ten words on the board in a random fashion: slippery, sharp, flickering, rustle, crash, shiver, trickled, birdsong, drips, dreamy. Arrange a selection of classroom instruments at the front of the class. Talk to the children about the music of words and how they often sound like the thing that they describe (see *Wet play*, page 7). Can they get the effect of the words in music? Spend some time experimenting. What happens when you combine some of the sounds?

3. Display the following:

   'Peering into the thicket, Jimmy could just make out the form of a small, bedraggled bird. It seemed to be caught in the thickest part of the hedge. Slowly and carefully he parted the drenched leaves and, clutching a branch with one hand, rustled forward to open the cage of slippery, tangled twigs with the other. Cold drips trickled down his neck. He shivered. Nearly there. Just ... one ... more ... With a sharp crack the branch gave way and Jimmy crashed headlong into the foliage. An exultant bird rose into the sky. Later, sleepy before a flickering fire, the boy dreamt of flight and freedom.'

Read the extract and ask the children how they could use instruments to accompany it. Take phrases like 'Cold drips trickled down his neck' and try out some of the sounds from activity 2. Create a band of five or six pupils to provide the incidental music. Give a performance to the class. (At first many of the children's ideas will sound like sound effects rather than incidental music; encourage them to create atmosphere as well as to mimic sounds. Over time their work will become broader and more thoughtful.)

Once they have created some incidental music for the story, ask them to play it without the words. Could you mould the sounds into a continuous piece that would capture the atmosphere created by the words? How could they use silence? Adapt the above approach to different age groups by changing the story. Fairytales work wonderfully well, or try extracts from the story you're reading now.

◎ Mime a rhyme

Sing three or four favourite nursery rhymes. Mime one of them for the children, but don't tell them which one. Try 'Little Miss Muffet' – eat your curds and whey and get nice and frightened. Which rhyme was it? Who would like to be Miss Muffet and who could be a scary spider? How does the spider move? Sing the rhyme while two children mime. Try the same technique with other songs that you've sung.

A chance to dance

1 Move from mime into dance – sing 'Here we go round the mulberry bush'. Ask ten pupils to join hands in a circle and to move round in time with the pulse. How can the actions of the song be transformed into a dance? How can the whole class be involved?

2 Many ballets have the most beautiful stories. Tell them the story of *Sleeping Beauty* and play them extracts from the ballet by Pyotr Ilyich Tchaikovsky.

3 *Coppelia* by Léo Delibes is the story of a young man who falls in love with a mechanical doll. One scene takes place in a workshop; all the mechanical dolls start to move. What would this look like? Who can be the best mechanical doll? Listen to some of the music.

Songs that tell a story

1 Discuss nursery rhyme stories in more detail. Why did Jack and Jill need water? Was it a very steep hill? Did Jack trip or was he pushed? How many stitches did he have? Was Jill hurt?

2 Have fun with some cumulative songs. Try 'There was an old lady who swallowed a fly'. When you get to the list, split it up with one child as each animal. The whole class then join in with the chorus. Discuss the song with them.

3 Try also 'The twelve days of Christmas' and 'One man went to mow'.

4 Listen to other songs that tell a story. Don't forget the old favourites; children are still spellbound by 'The ugly duckling' and 'The King's new clothes', Danny Kaye. Older children will love 'Hello Muddah, hello Fuddah', Allan Sherman; and 'Right, said Fred', Bernard Cribbins.

Look for narrative folk songs and ballads from around the world. From the 60s, try 'Yellow submarine', 'Maxwell's silver hammer' and 'Eleanor Rigby', The Beatles; 'Sloop John B', The Beach Boys; anything by Joan Baez or Fairport Convention. 'Ode to Billy Joe', Bobby Gentry, will get a good discussion going with your top juniors. What happened to Billy Joe?

MC and Rap are often narrative, but be careful – check the language and subject matter thoroughly before you play it to the class!

Music and stories

1 Composer Nikolay Rimsky-Korsakov's orchestral suite *Scheherazade* is based on tales from 'The Arabian Nights'. Sinbad the Sailor is featured in the first movement; 'The sea and Sinbad's ship'. You may wish to approach the music through one of the many Sinbad adventure stories that are available.

2 Listen to Sergei Prokofiev's *Peter and the Wolf* at home and tell your pupils the story. Which instruments would they use for the cat, the duck and the wolf? How do these animals move? What about Grandfather or Peter? What would the music be like? Have some instruments ready. Can they show you? Now play them the recording.

3 Listen to some recordings of music from recent films; see if the children can tell you what was happening in the film. With Disney's classic *Fantasia*, play a sequence of the video with the sound turned down. What do they think the music would be like? Then turn the volume up.

Sports day

13/14 Sports day samba

With great energy, but not too fast!

Let's do the sports day samba, get those muscles pump-in', feel your heart a-thump-in', sports day samba, shake those la-zy old bones. Let's do the sports day samba, keep your breath-ing stea-dy, now you're near-ly rea-dy, sports day samba, count to three and let's go!

FINE

1. Egg and spoon race, pret-ty trick-y, palms are sweat-ing, fin-gers stick-y, Now the re-lay, such di-sa-ster, legs just won't go a-ny fast-er. Crowd is cheer-ing, flags are fly-ing, ev-'ry-one is real-ly try-ing, Jam-ie's fal-len, Tom is win-ning, see his team, they can't stop grin-ning! Let's do the

2. Now the high jump, mus-cles ach-ing, points to win and re-cords break-ing, As you're sprint-ing down the track now hold your course and don't look back now. Hands are clap-ping, whis-tles blow-ing, breath-ing stea-dy, pulse is slow-ing, What a tri-umph, such e-la-tion, now there'll be a ce-le-bra-tion! Let's do the

D.S. al Fine

19

Egg-and-spoon race

In an egg-and-spoon race, the child must get to the finishing line first without dropping the egg. In music it is sometimes very hard not to drop a beat.

Form a circle. Teach the pupils a rhythm that they must clap or tap steadily. If you are unsure which rhythm to use, take one from a nursery rhyme (you don't have to tell your Year 5s where it's from!). Try the rhythm of 'pitter patter raindrops' (just that line), until the children are confident. Tell them that you are going to do everything in your power to make them drop the beat. Start them off all clapping together and go round the circle playing completely different rhythms right in front of each child on a tambourine. The object is to get as many of the children to drop the beat (egg) as possible, leaving you with a winner or winners.

Long jump/short jump

Just as it is possible to jump a long way and then make short jumps, so in music there are long notes and shorter ones. Sing a favourite song together and find the longest notes and shortest notes. What is the prize-winning long note?

Take a note or sustainable sound and ask the children to follow your hand signals. Conduct long and short sounds with your hands.

For the high jump!

Sing a song that you all know and talk about the jumps between notes. Are there any particularly big leaps (for example, the first two notes of 'My bonny lies over the ocean')? Which jump is the biggest, gold-medal-winning leap?

Relay

In a relay race it is vital that the baton is passed on smoothly with the minimum of hesitation. In music teamwork can also be crucial. Just as timing is important to the change over of the baton, so it is when an instrument enters a piece of music. If they come in at the wrong tempo, or slightly too late, the beat (baton) will be dropped.

Form a circle. The teacher must tap a steady pulse on a drum, tambour or tambourine. Say 'walk, walk, walk, walk' as the rhythm is tapped. Ask each child in turn around the circle to tap 'run-ning'; one 'run-ning' to each of your 'walks'. The children's 'run-ning' must fit continuously with your pulse; if any child falters they are dropping the baton (**CD track 15**)!

Children:	Run-ning	Run-ning	Run-ning	Run-ning
Teacher:	Walk	Walk	Walk	Walk

As the pupils get quicker the game becomes more challenging; they can start with the 400-metre relay, progress to the 200 and graduate to the sprint relay! When they become really good at this try harder rhythms (see 'Carnival!' in *Ceremonies and special occasions*, page 32).

Up tempo/down beat

Sing a nursery rhyme or song that the pupils know well and discuss how the choice of speed can alter its mood or character. Just as runners will find the right race for their talents – marathon, 100 metres, 1500 metres – so a song has the right tempo (speed) for its meaning. What else effects your choice of tempo? Are there some rhythms that just don't work faster or slower? How about the words?

Football crazy!

Take names of well-known football teams and see if the children can clap their rhythms:

    Manchester United   West Ham   Everton

Put two teams together – a fixture (**track 16**)! Try Manchester United v. Everton! See if they can identify the team just from the rhythm. In pairs, ask the children to invent their own fixtures. When they play them to the class, the audience must identify which teams they are.

Practice makes perfect

Discuss the idea of 'practice' with the children. Sportsmen and women and musicians all have to practise; it takes years of hard work to excel. Open up the issue of talent and today's pop stars. Do they practise hard?

Sports themes

There are numerous examples of sports themes that have been associated with different sporting events. There are many good compilation CDs with collections of these themes. Have a short quiz, asking the children to name some of the themes. Why were they chosen?

Tongue gymnastics!

Tongue twisters are very good for speech and rhythm development and great fun. Try these two:

'There was a fisherman named Fisher,
Who fished for some fish in a fissure.
'Til a fish with a grin,
Pulled the fisherman in,
Now they're fishing the fissure for Fisher'.

'Wun-wun was a racehorse,
Tutu was one two.
Wun-wun won one race,
Tutu won one two'.

The art of sport

There are some sports that come very close to the arts. Ice-skating and gymnastics both use music. Discuss this with the children. Ice-skating and dance are very close, yet one is a sport and one an art. Why?

Dinner queue

17 Lunchtime rap

In a performance of this rap, try experimenting with different dynamics (volume).

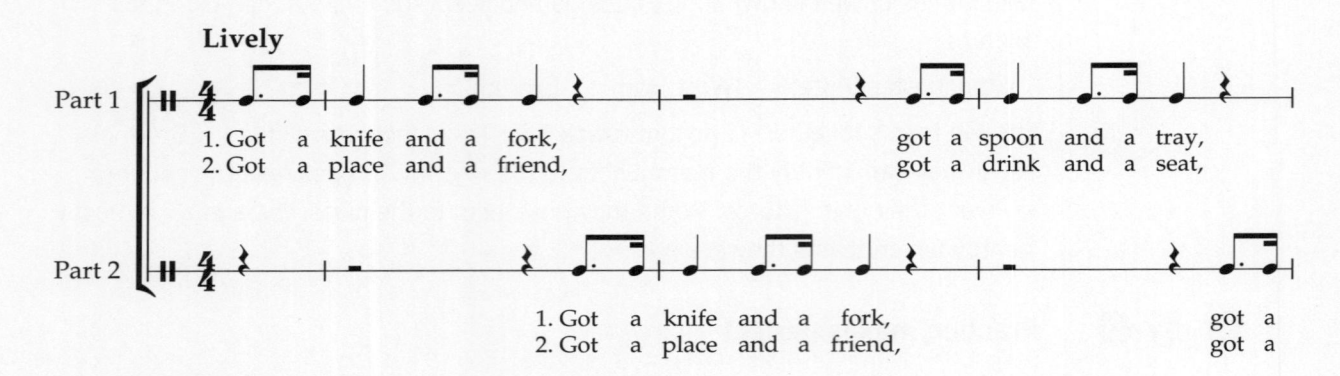

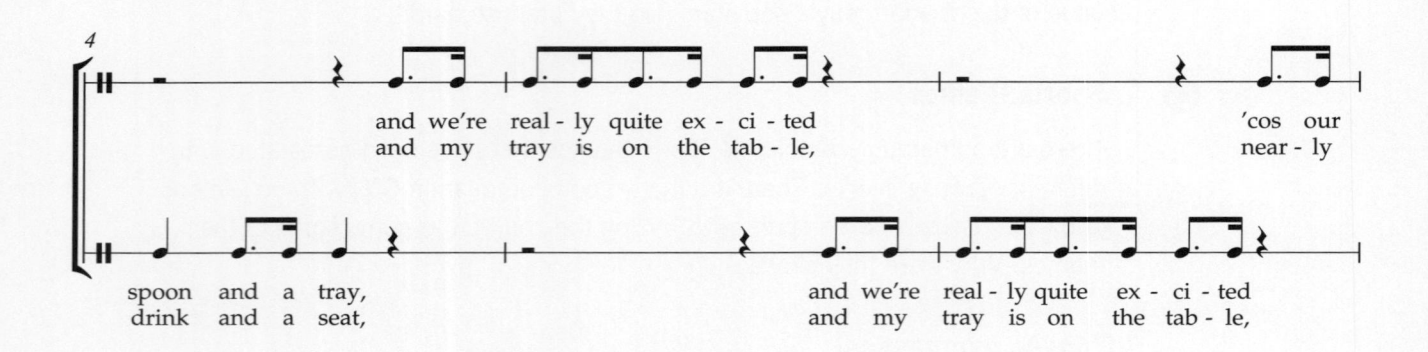

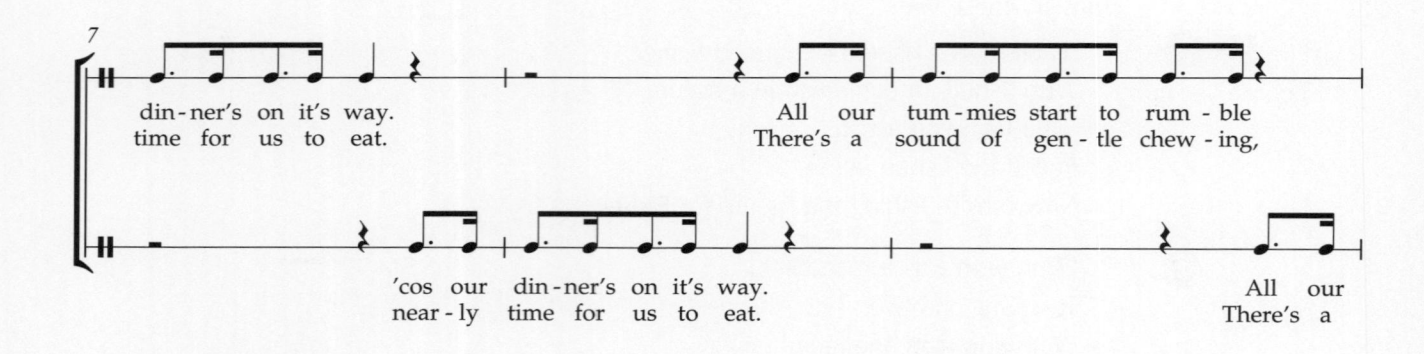

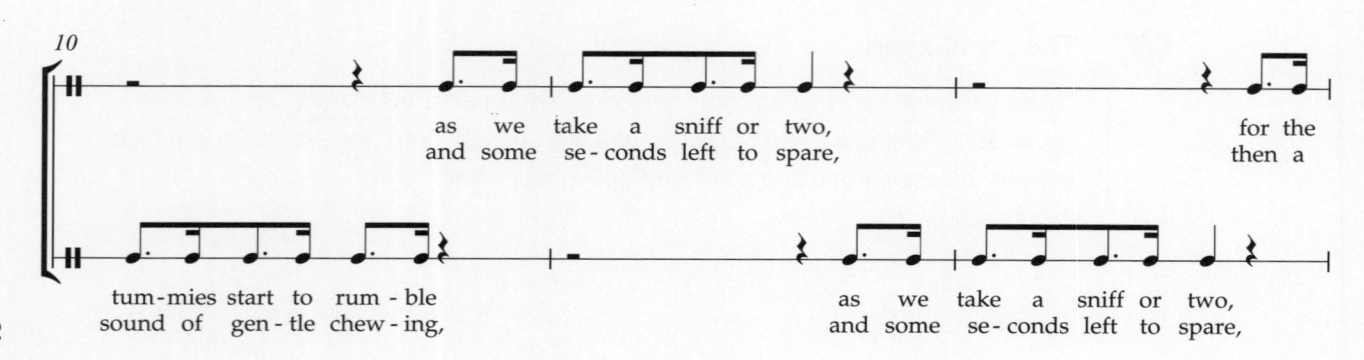

Lively

Part 1:
1. Got a knife and a fork, got a spoon and a tray, and we're really quite excited 'cos our dinner's on it's way. All our tummies start to rumble as we take a sniff or two, for the

2. Got a place and a friend, got a drink and a seat, and my tray is on the table, nearly time for us to eat. There's a sound of gentle chewing, and some seconds left to spare, then a

Part 2:
1. Got a knife and a fork, got a spoon and a tray, and we're really quite excited 'cos our dinner's on it's way. All our tummies start to rumble as we take a sniff or two,

2. Got a place and a friend, got a drink and a seat, and my tray is on the table, nearly time for us to eat. There's a sound of gentle chewing, and some seconds left to spare,

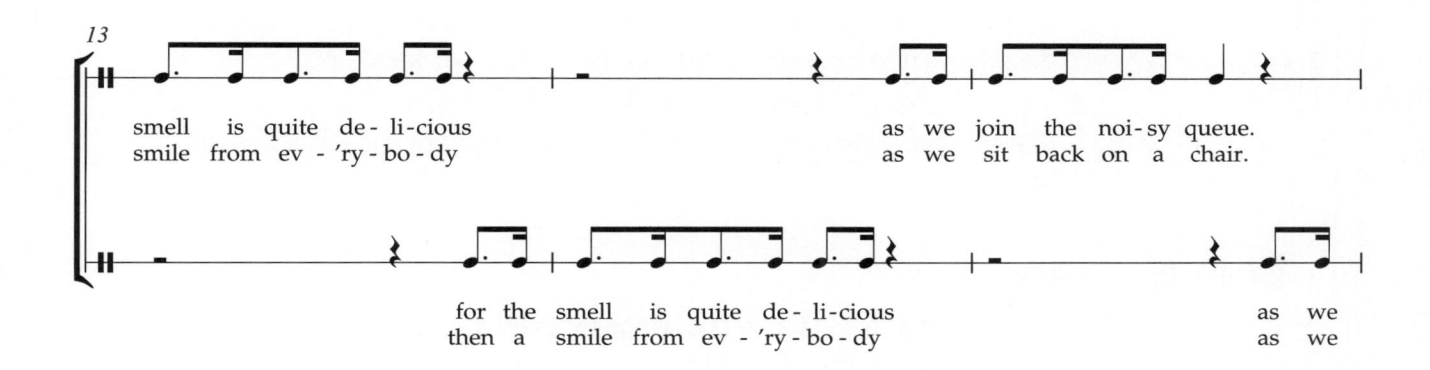

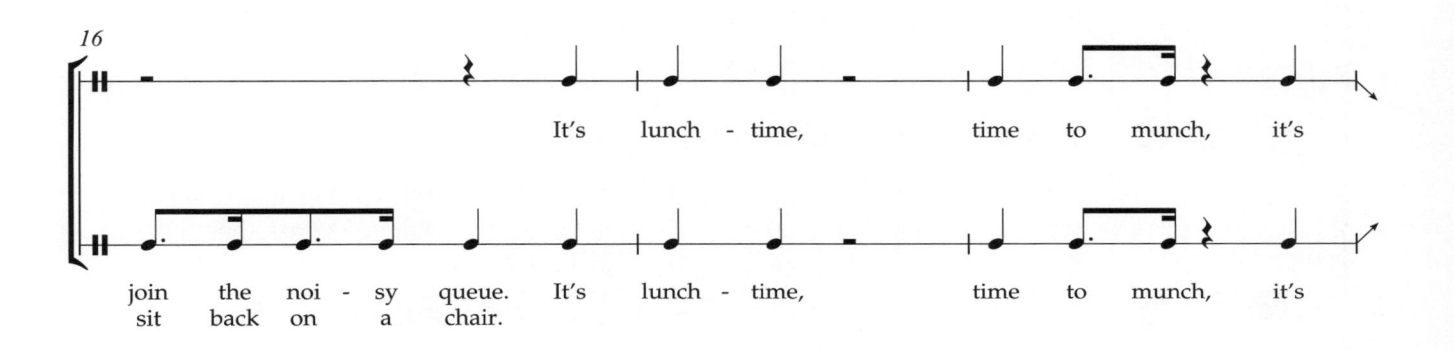

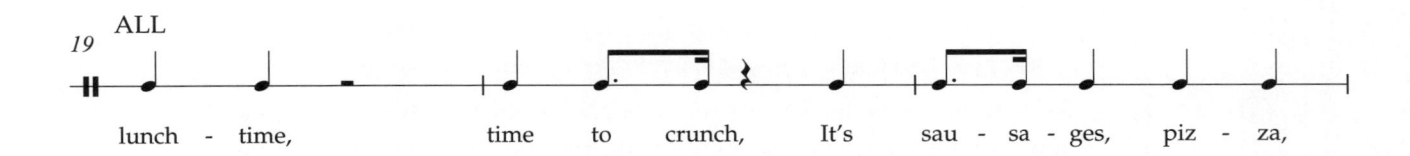

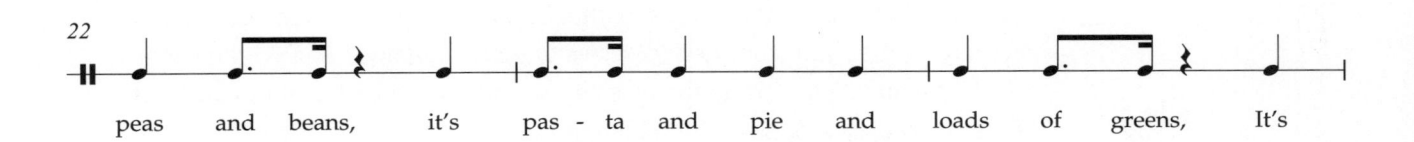

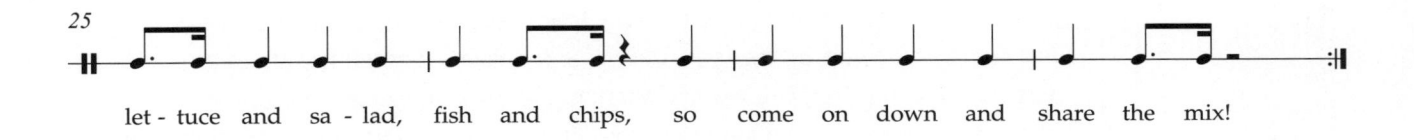

13
smell is quite de-li-cious   as we join the noi-sy queue.
smile from ev-'ry-bo-dy   as we sit back on a chair.

         for the smell is quite de-li-cious   as we
         then a smile from ev-'ry-bo-dy   as we

16
                        It's lunch-time,   time to munch, it's
join the noi-sy queue. It's lunch-time,   time to munch, it's
sit back on a chair.

19 ALL
lunch-time,   time to crunch, It's sau-sa-ges, piz-za,

22
peas and beans, it's pas-ta and pie and loads of greens, It's

25
let-tuce and sa-lad, fish and chips, so come on down and share the mix!

Utensil rap!

1 Collect a series of utensils from your kitchen; forks, spoons, a few old glasses and plates, a cheese-grater, jars, saucepans ... Experiment with the objects, using them as percussion instruments. Draw comparisons with 'proper' percussion. Tell the children that the percussion section of an orchestra is nicknamed 'the kitchen' by other players. Why do they think this is?

2 Fill the glasses with different levels of water and 'ping' them lightly with a hard beater. If you can find some glass milk bottles, even better! Compare the pitches of the sounds. What can the children say about this?

3 Find a recording of someone playing the spoons. Can anyone work out how to play a simple rhythm on a couple of spoons? Compare the spoons with some castanets.

Wrap rap!

We all discard a mountain of food wrapping every day. Using crisp packets, plastic bottles, cartons, cellophane wrapping and yoghurt pots, demonstrate a range of sounds. Ask for volunteers to play a rhythm on one of the items. Could four or five play a rhythm piece together? Could they accompany *Lunchtime rap*?

If music be the food ...

Composing music and preparing food share some vocabulary: mixing, blending, texture, layering, ingredients ... Point this out to the children and ask them why they think this is. We even talk of a 'taste' in music!

1 Lay out a varied selection of four or five different percussion instruments at the front of the class. These are the ingredients. Two volunteers must choose two and put them in the blender, i.e. play them together. Try three, four or even five instruments together. Do they blend well? Is the texture smooth or lumpy? How could they get a smoother or lumpier texture?

2 Try a blind tasting! The instruments are hidden from the class's view. The volunteers must play the instruments and the class must identify the ingredients.

3 Can the class make up a sandwich using words from 'Lunchtime rap'? Try 'sausages, pizza, sausages, pizza' without a break between each pair. Clap it first, saying it as you clap. Ask the class to join in quietly. Then do the same with 'fish and chips'. Divide the class in two and try them together (**CD track 18**). It should be a popular combination!

What's on the menu?

Draw the children's attention to the way that menus are balanced; you have a light starter, followed by the main course and dessert. Sometimes there are more courses, but they are usually contrasting. Similarly, classical concert programmes are balanced carefully. You often have an overture, followed by one or two main courses and an encore. Even pieces of music have contrasting movements (courses). Listen to pieces such as *Carnival of the Animals*, Camille Saint-Saëns, or *The Planets*, Gustav Holst and note the contrasts.

Musical digest

Listen to some of J.S. Bach's *Coffee Cantata* 211, which he wrote in praise of coffee. Then listen to 'Food, glorious food' from Lionel Bart's *Oliver*. Which food would the children write music in praise of? What would the music be like?

Don't know your rap from your MC?

There's a bewildering number of different musical styles that use rap and variations of it; Rap, MC, Hip-hop, Drum 'n' bass, Jungle etc. Ask the children to do some research on the internet and to share their findings with the class. What are the differences between these styles?

Blending the ingredients

Combine your 'utensils music' and the 'wrap rhythms' to provide a rhythmic accompaniment to a performance of 'Lunchtime rap'.

Builders in school

The building song

Allegretto

1. The tea-chers said "We've got no room, we've got no room at all! Can't fit them in, we're in a spin, we need to make some more. But how can we af-ford this work, what-e-ver must we pay? We'll have to raise the mo-ney and we'll do it straight a-way. We'll build a place, a ve-ry big space where all of us can be, A place of our own which feels like home where there's room for you and me!

2. The plan-ners came and drew a plan, the pa-per-work was done, The tea-chers said with nod-ding heads "Oh won't all this be fun!" Then build-ers came with lor-ry and crane and bricks and mor-tar too, With scaf-fold poles and great big holes, there was so much work to do.

3. We watched it grow-ing day by day, with win-dows, tiles and doors, We watched the plas-ter 'til it dried and saw the woo-den floor. Then paint was brushed up-on the walls, it all looked fresh and new, 'Til fi-nal-ly this space you see was rea-dy for me and you.

room for you and me!

Layer upon layer

Take lines from the song and build a rhythm piece. Chant the line 'we watched it growing day by day' five or six times with the class, without pausing at the end of the line. Encourage the children to speak distinctly and rhythmically, without shouting.

Do the same with 'we'll build a place, a very big space' and 'a place of our own which feels like home'. When you are confident that the children can do this well, divide the class into two. Start group 1 with 'we watched it growing ...' and once they are steady, bring in group 2 with 'we'll build a place ...'. Then swap the rhythms over.

Once the children can perform confidently in two groups, divide them into three and add 'a place of our own which feels like home'.

Discuss with the class ways that you could make the piece more varied and interesting. 'We watched it growing day by day' could start quietly and gradually get louder towards the end of the line (a *crescendo*). 'We'll build a space' could be whispered, and 'a very big space' chanted loudly.

One day the building surveyor comes in and says that the construction is going too slowly. Could the piece go faster? Could it start slowly and get quicker? The neighbours have complained that the building work is too noisy. Try whispering the piece.

When the children are confident with this activity, introduce instruments.

Mouth mime

If you want to improve the pupils' diction when they are singing, try this: Ask them to imagine that there is a soundproof window between you and them (like in a recording studio). Mouth a line and see if they can tell which one it is. Make one deliberately indistinct so that you can then discuss why they couldn't tell which line it was. Put the children in pairs and ask them to mime lines to each other. Ask for volunteers to mouth mime a line in front of the class. Now sing *The building song* again and listen to the improvement!

Building site

Brainstorm words connected with building. These words could be:
- Implements (nails/hammers/sandpaper)
- Materials (steel/gravel/water/cement)
- People (bricklayer/carpenter/builder)
- Sounds (shuka, shuka/bang, bang/tika tika, whoosh/whoosh)

Give different groups a word to chant and build a piece using three or four words:

	1	2	3	4
1.	Nails	Nails	Nails	Nails
2.	Hammer	Hammer	Hammer	Hammer
3.	Sandpaper	Sandpaper	Sandpaper	Sandpaper
4.	Shukashuka	Shukashuka	Shukashuka	Shukashuka

Divide the pupils into groups of four and ask them to compose work rhythm pieces in the same way, using any of the words on the board and/or some of their own. Remind them that the dynamic (volume) and tempo (speed) can be varied. Can they think of any actions that would fit the sounds?

Hear the pieces back. What would happen if all the pieces were played at once (a building site)? Use some of the pieces to accompany 'The building song'.

Sound materials

Good pieces of music combine different materials, just like a strong building. Using classroom percussion, select ten wooden instruments (wood blocks, claves, xylophones); ten metal ones (triangles, metallophones, chime bars, bells); ten with skins (tambours, drums). Give the instruments out so that the children are grouped according to metal, wood and skin. Using some of the words from 'Building site' (above), build a rhythm piece with the three groups. The metal could tap 'Nails, nails'; the wood 'Hammer, hammer'; the skins 'Sandpaper'. A few maracas would make a very good 'Shuka, shuka'.

Builders' union

In order for this building to be finished on time, good industrial relations are essential. Can the builders in your class work in harmony? Try this.

With half the class, start to sing the song but freeze on 'Tea -' of teachers; the second note. (So the children sing 'The teeeeeeeeeeeeeeeeeeeeeeeeeeee'). Tell them to hold the note on but to breathe when they feel like it. With the other half, sing 'The teachers sai – '; freezing on the 'sai' of said. They will enjoy the harmony.

Sound architects

Draw some shapes on the board (circles, curves, dots, squares, angles, lines, spirals). Take a tambourine and see if you can interpret some of them in sound. Ask some volunteers to draw some shapes and play them. Could the children design a simple building and then play it?

Display the designs. Can you tell which one belongs to which piece? Give one pupil's design to another and ask them to play it. Bring in some photos or posters of famous buildings. Could you 'play' them? Try the Guggenheim in Bilbao, the Millennium bridge, the Eiffel Tower …

Listening to building

Most music builds and develops. The following pieces illustrate this particularly clearly: *Drumming*, Steve Reich; *Bolero*, Maurice Ravel; 'The Boxer' (the final wordless chorus) from *Bridge over troubled water*, Simon and Garfunkel; any fugue from the 48 Preludes and Fugues by J.S. Bach; Kodo drumming; *Adagio for strings*, Samuel Barber; *The Rite of Spring* (opening), Igor Stravinsky.

Add to the list with recordings from your own collection of CDs and discuss with your pupils how the music builds and develops.

Computers

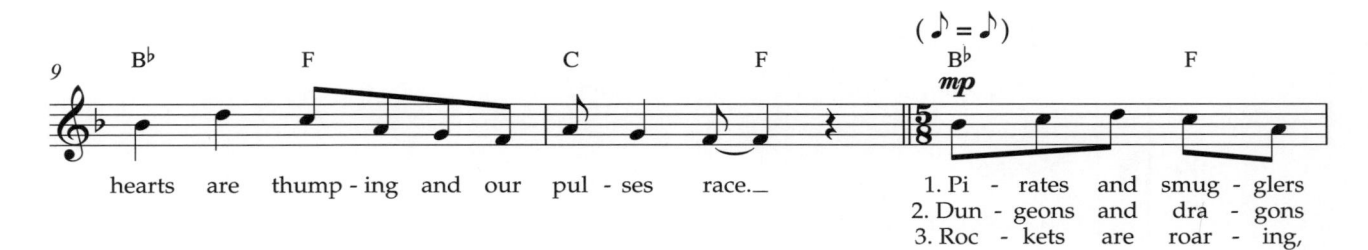

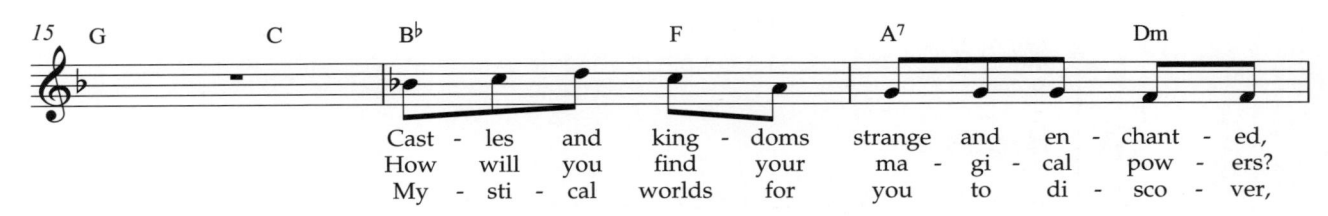

Computer crazy 21/22

Not too fast!

We're all go-ing com-pu-ter cra-zy, the screens are flash-ing, we're on the case,__ We're all go-ing com-pu-ter cra-zy, our hearts are thump-ing and our pul-ses race.__

4th time to Coda

1. Pi - rates and smug - glers cross-ing the o-cean, em-pires to con-quer, cit-ies to win,
2. Dun - geons and dra - gons hide in the dark-ness, guard-ing the trea-sure deep in a cave,
3. Roc - kets are roar - ing, en - gines are rac - ing, steer-ing your space-ship in-to the skies,

Cast-les and king-doms strange and en-chant-ed, spells to un-tan-gle, quests to be-gin.
How will you find your ma-gi-cal pow-ers? Can you be dar-ing, cle-ver and brave?
My-sti-cal worlds for you to dis-co-ver, a-li-en be-ings wait to sur-prise!

repeat three times

CODA

hearts are thump-ing and our pul-ses race.__

It's all in the game

1 Computer games use sound effects and music to help create atmosphere. Talk to the children about the difference between a sound effect and music (see *Wet play*, page 6 and *Telling a story*, page 17). With a few percussion instruments, make some sound effects – how could a wood block become a grandfather clock, or maracas be someone walking up the drive? Then play a recording of some famous high-tension music; try the music from *Jaws* or *Psycho* (they don't have to know the full story!).

2 Find a colourful two-page spread from a comic book that has plenty of 'boings', 'biffs' and 'kerrrangs'. Your pupils will be only too keen to help you find a good example! Show it to the class and ask individual children to make the sounds using their voices and mouths. Play a recording of Cathy Berberian singing *Stripsody*.

3 Divide the pupils into groups of three or four and give each group a small but varied selection of percussion instruments. Ask them to devise a short computer game with sound effects. They could use an idea from the song:

'Pirates and smugglers crossing the ocean'
'Castles and kingdoms strange and enchanted'
'Dungeons and dragons hide in the darkness'
'Rockets are roaring, engines are racing'

Mouse!

Most studios, portable or otherwise, can make sounds echo. At story time, sit five pupils in a circle. Pupil 1 shouts 'mouse', followed by pupil 2 shouting slightly less loudly, pupil 3 even less and so on. Try to get the repetitions steady and the degrees of quietness spread evenly across the five. Then try it with ten pupils.

Key in to music

There are many excellent computer music games that educate well and are great fun. When your pupils are catching up on project work or engaged in different activities, send a couple of children over to the computer to try one.

Home studio

Computer technology is used extensively in the professional music recording industry and there are also a number of excellent software programmes that can give you a virtual recording studio at home. You can link a music keyboard to your computer and record your own tracks to quite a sophisticated level of recording quality. There have been several examples of Top Ten discs that were created and recorded by musicians in this way. Talk to your pupils about this and find out if any of them have parents or older brothers or sisters who use a computer to make music.

Mixing it

In recording studios there is usually some kind of mixing desk, which allows the sound engineer to balance the sound and to add special effects. In multi-track recording, the different musicians in a group are recorded on separate tracks; sound levels on individual tracks can be adjusted separately.

Draw your own version of a mixing desk on a large piece of paper so that you can use it again and again. Try this:

Mixing desk volume

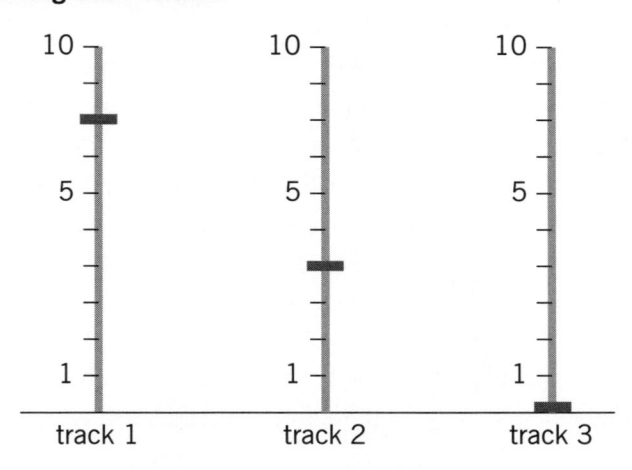

1 Divide the class into three. Track 1 is group 1, track 2 – group 2, and so on. Ask group 1 to chant 'Hard disk, hard disk, hard disk' steadily. Point to track 1. As your finger rises or falls the group must follow the volume level (without getting faster or slower!). At '1' they should be whispering. If you go down to the line they should mouth the words noiselessly. Group 2 chants 'multi-track' and group 3 'playstation'. For example (**CD track 23**):

Track 1:	Hard disk	Hard Disk	Hard Disk
Track 2:	Multi-track	Multi-track	Multi-track
Track 3:	Playstation	Playstation	Playstation

Vary the volume of each group at will.

2 Invite a pupil to move the controls.

3 Instead of vocal chanting, have shaking clusters of instruments on each track – for example, bells on 1, tambourines on 2 and maracas on 3.

Sound bytes

Japanese musician Tomita created some magical arrangements of well-known classical pieces using synthesisers and computer technology. Any of his recordings will stimulate a lively debate about whether computers and synthesisers could ever replace traditional acoustic instruments. Play music from his album of *The Planets*, Gustav Holst and compare it with the orchestral version.

Ceremonies and special occasions

Carnival!

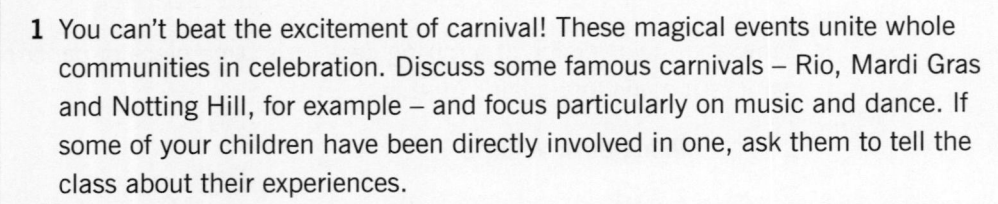

1. You can't beat the excitement of carnival! These magical events unite whole communities in celebration. Discuss some famous carnivals – Rio, Mardi Gras and Notting Hill, for example – and focus particularly on music and dance. If some of your children have been directly involved in one, ask them to tell the class about their experiences.

2. What kind of music would you expect to hear at a carnival? It must surely be music you can dance and move to. Build up a rhythm in layers, according to the ages and abilities of your pupils. Look at 'Relay' in *Sports day* (page 20) and practise clapping 'walk' and 'run-ning' with the whole class, alternating between the two. Then divide the class into two. Start group one with 'walk' and then introduce group two's 'run-ning'. Is the tempo (speed) right for marching and dancing? Ask your pupils to decide which tempo works best. Try a very fast one and a very slow one. What are they learning about good carnival music? Challenge older pupils with some more difficult rhythms. Have three groups (layers). Try 'walk' and 'running' and add 'top banana' (**CD track 24**).

3. Listen to *Sports day samba* on the CD (**track 13**) and sing it with the children. Try clapping 'walk', 'running' and 'top banana' above the piano track. To begin with, ask the pupils to say the words as they clap. When it's secure, see if it's possible to walk and dance to it. Can a group sing the song while the rhythm group walks and claps? If you had a *Sports day samba* float in the main parade, what would be on it?

4. Could the children get together a float based on a nursery rhyme? What about *Humpty Dumpty*? What would be on the float? Can you make a huge Humpty Dumpty? Or should he be in pieces? What about the wall? Who are going to be the King's horses and men?

5. March around the room singing the rhyme. Can some drummers tap '1, 2, sat on a wall' (same as '1, 2, buckle my shoe') over and over again while the song is sung and the King's men ride in?

6. Listen to some carnival music or watch a video clip. Which classroom instruments will give the best carnival sound? Experiment. Try different instruments with the rhythms you developed in activities 2 and 3.

Religious ceremony

Talk to your pupils about the way music is used in religious ceremony. It's hard to imagine a celebration of Christmas, for example, without music. As well as the carols and festive music sung and played in church services, you'll hear carol singers in the streets and seasonal music on the TV and radio.

Music is important in many religions. If you have pupils from a range of cultural heritages ask them to tell the class about the role that music plays within their traditions. What kind of music is played at a Sikh wedding, Hanukkah or Diwali? Ask two or three pupils to carry out some research on the internet. Find some CDs of the music and listen to them in class.

Which music is appropriate for a wedding? See if your children can tell you what they think would be suitable. You certainly wouldn't have sad music! What would they choose?

Time machine

Set your time machine and find out how music has been used in celebrations across the centuries. Here are some ideas:

1 Listen to *La Mourisque* by Tylman Susato and imagine a party at a Tudor court! Tudor dance music often had a tambour or hand drum tapping a repeated rhythm (ostinato). Who can tap steadily to the recording?

2 Despite his fearsome reputation, Henry VIII was actually a cultured and very musical monarch. He played several instruments and composed, although it is difficult to be sure which pieces were actually written by him. The song *Pastime with good companye* is attributed to Henry VIII and is great fun to sing with older pupils. Use some light percussion to accompany the singing.

3 In 1749 King George II asked the composer George Frideric Handel to write some music to celebrate the signing of the Treaty of Aix-la-Chapelle. Handel composed the wonderful *Music for the Royal Fireworks*, although at the performance one of the pavilions caught fire! Handel's Firework Music contains dance music and is meant to accompany the fireworks, not to sound like them. Listen to 'La rejouissance' ('rejoicing') and imagine the scene. Ask the children to suggest other pieces of music that would go well with fireworks.

4 At the Coronation of Queen Elizabeth II in 1953 the glorious music was one of the highlights of the ceremony. What qualities would the children expect coronation music to have? Listen to some of the music or watch a video clip of the service in Westminster Abbey.

5 Music was very much a feature of the Queen's Golden Jubilee celebrations in 2002. There were religious services, military bands, children's performances and the two extraordinary concerts – one pop and one classical – in the grounds of Buckingham Palace. Compare the way music was used in the Coronation and Golden Jubilee celebrations. There has been a remarkable change in society's attitude to popular music over the last 50 years! Discuss this with the children.

Military music

1 With younger pupils, sing 'The grand old Duke of York'. Put together a small marching band with some tambourines, tambours, drums and woodblocks, and play some of the rhythms from the song over a steady basic marching pulse. Sing, march and play (but don't ask the children to march while they are playing recorders! A slight trip can turn into a very nasty accident). Can you march more quickly? More slowly?

2 Find some CDs or video clips of military bands and play them to the children. What are the main characteristics of a good military piece? What is the music for? What would happen if a march was played too quickly, or if the rhythm was uneven? Why are the instruments usually brass, woodwind and percussion? Why are there no violins or cellos?

There's a bee in the classroom!

I can hear a bee!

In a performance of this round, try experimenting with different dynamics (volume).

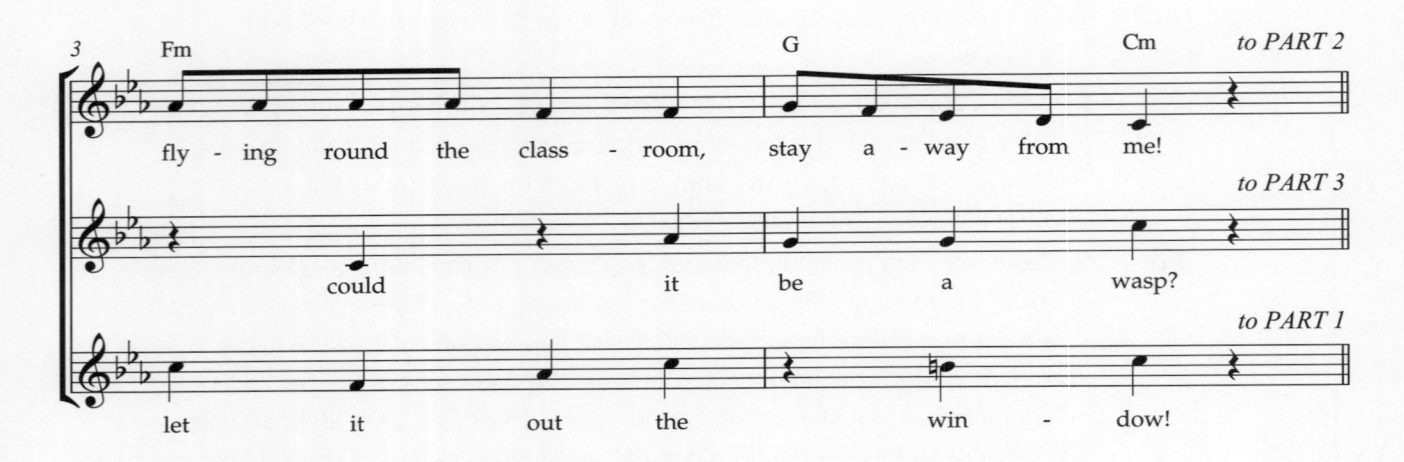

At a moderate speed

Part 1: Bzz bzz, I can hear a bee

Part 2: Keep still, there's a bzz bzz,

Part 3: Gent - ly, bzz bzz

Part 1: fly - ing round the class - room, stay a - way from me! *to PART 2*

Part 2: could it be a wasp? *to PART 3*

Part 3: let it out the win - dow! *to PART 1*

Waxing lyrical

Talk about the words of the song, drawing particular attention to 'bzz'. Discuss how the actual sounds of things have become words. 'Bzz' has become the buzzing of a bee or any buzz; the 'sss' of a snake is called a hiss, a dog 'barks', cats 'miaou' … How many can they think of? Could they write some words for a song about a snake? Try some other creatures, using *I can hear a bee!* as a model.

Drones

A drone has a particular role to play in bee society. There are also drones in music. Bagpipes have drones that produce an underlying tone to the melody and there are drones – low, continuous notes – in other kinds of music. Can anyone 'buzz' a low drone while the rest of the class sing the song? Find a recording of some bagpipe music and see if the children can identify the drone.

The flight of the bumble bee

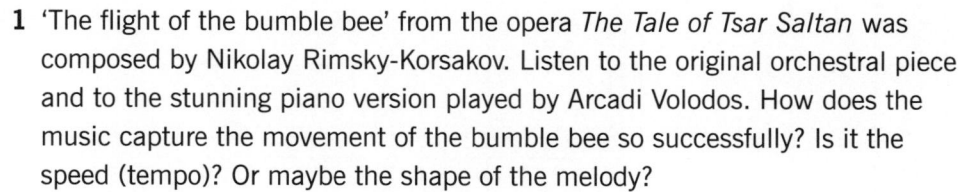

1 'The flight of the bumble bee' from the opera *The Tale of Tsar Saltan* was composed by Nikolay Rimsky-Korsakov. Listen to the original orchestral piece and to the stunning piano version played by Arcadi Volodos. How does the music capture the movement of the bumble bee so successfully? Is it the speed (tempo)? Or maybe the shape of the melody?

2 Draw the flight path of a bumble bee on the board. Ask one pupil to come to the front and trace the path on the board with a ruler. Invite volunteers to vary the pitch of their buzz as the flight is traced up and down across the board. Point out that traditional music notation is based on the principle of the higher the symbol on the page, the higher the sound.

Hive of industry

Sit the children in a circle. Send a 'buzz' round the circle, passing it on with a light touch on the arm. Try sending it as quickly as possible. When the first buzz is half way round, send another one, at a different pitch. Can they do three?

Royal jelly

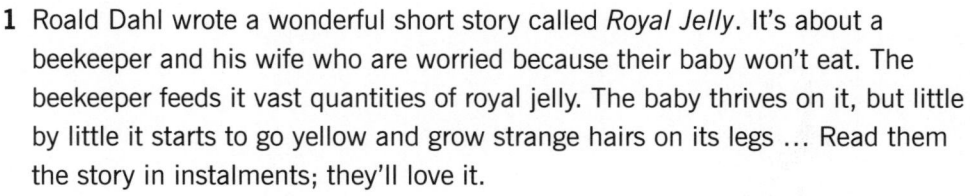

1 Roald Dahl wrote a wonderful short story called *Royal Jelly*. It's about a beekeeper and his wife who are worried because their baby won't eat. The beekeeper feeds it vast quantities of royal jelly. The baby thrives on it, but little by little it starts to go yellow and grow strange hairs on its legs … Read them the story in instalments; they'll love it.

2 Are there any episodes in the story that they could invent some music for? What kinds of sounds could they make: a) with their mouths and voices and b) with instruments? How can they get the effect of rapid but rather weird growth? If you only have a short time, experiment with a few instruments at the front of the class, trying out their suggestions. There is plenty of material here for a longer composing project!

Late for school

26 Late again

In a performance of this round, try experimenting with different dynamics (volume).

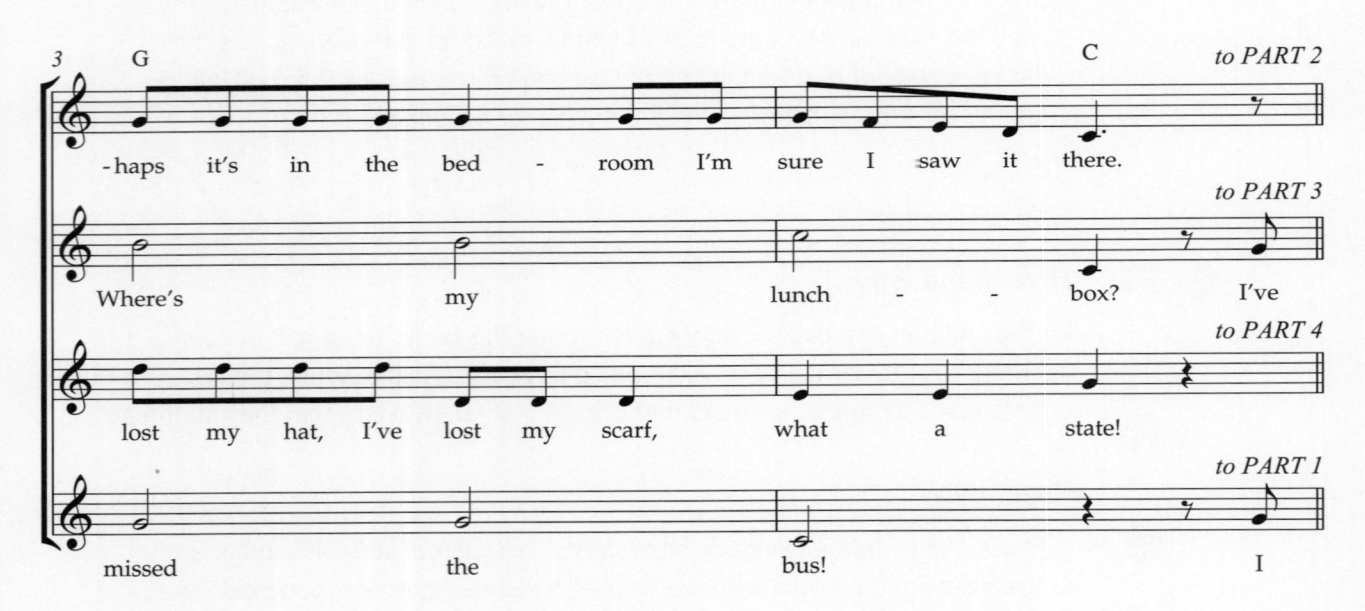

At a moderate speed

Part 1: I can't find my school-bag, I put it down some-where, Per-haps it's in the bed-room I'm sure I saw it there.

Part 2: Where's my lunch-box? Where's my lunch-box? I've

Part 3: I've lost my coat, I've lost my gloves and now I'm late, I've lost my hat, I've lost my scarf, what a state!

Part 4: What a fuss I've missed the bus! I

On the dot

1 Sit the pupils in a circle. Ask them to imagine a ticking clock and clap the ticking yourself – 'tick, tock, tick, tock'. Point out how steady a ticking clock is. Who can join in? Ask all the pupils to clap and say 'tick, tock'; clap first on one side and then the other to give the idea of a pendulum swinging in time. Once a steady pulse has been established, call out the following phrases from the song in time with the ticking:

Tick	Tock	Tick	Tock
Lost my coat	Lost my gloves	Lost my hat	Lost my scarf

2 Ask half the class to clap the 'tick, tocks' and the other half to clap and chant 'lost my coat, lost my gloves, lost my hat, lost my scarf'. Each 'lost' must come on a 'tick' or a 'tock' – on the dot (**CD track 27**)!

3 Try and double the tempo (speed) of the ticking (**CD track 28**). Try and alternate between the slow tempo and the faster one.

Action song

Could the children make up their own actions to go with the song? What would the actions be for 'I've lost my coat/gloves/hat/scarf'? Ask them to work out an action routine in pairs or small groups. The actions must be on time! Choose the best to try with the whole class.

Count me in

Coming in on time is essential when you're making music. You have to listen carefully, stay alert, count and watch the conductor. If you miss your entry in music you've had it; you can't catch the next bus! Sing any song with an accompaniment (piano or CD) and deliberately bring the children in at the wrong place. Chaos will ensue! Talk to them about why it sounds so chaotic; rhythms not fitting, clashing harmonies … Then bring them in at the right time. If you're singing a round such as *Late again* or *I can hear a bee!*, what happens if one of the parts comes in late?

Bang on time

1 Choose four or five pupils and give them tambourines, tambours, hand drums or wood blocks; any instrument that can make a short sound. Raise your hands and bring them down, stopping suddenly at a precise point. Ask the pupils to play when you stop at this point. See if you can get them to play at precisely the same time. They will begin to understand that they need to get ready to play when you raise your hands. To start with, perform the gesture regularly. Try it with one hand. When they are used to your beat, introduce some irregularity and see if they can follow you. Can one of the pupils be the conductor? Change the instrumentalists each time you do this.

2 Find a recording of the Fifth Symphony, Jean Sibelius. The final chords of the symphony, right at the end of the last movement, are notoriously difficult to get right. Play the ending to the children and ask them why they think it is so difficult. Imagine if even one player was late!

3 Tell them a famous musicians' modern myth. Percussionists sometimes have

only one or two sounds to make on a particular instrument. One unfortunate musician had two triangle 'tings' to play towards the end of a twenty-minute piece of music and had to count and watch the conductor carefully. The conductor forgot to bring him in and in the end the poor player missed the 'tings' altogether!

Listening time

Listen to the second movement of Symphony No.101 in D, the 'Clock', Franz Joseph Haydn, and draw the children's attention to the persistent, clock-like rhythm that gave the piece its nickname. Try also *The Syncopated Clock*, Leroy Anderson and *Time Piece*, Paul Patterson.

Dennis the Digital Watch

Tell the story of Dennis the Digital Watch:

'Poor Dennis was fed up. He'd given his owner years of service but was always getting blamed for being late. Sometimes he was shaken or even given a sharp tap. He knew he had a bit of a problem with being on time and he always did his best, but somehow he was always just that little bit behind. The Clocks were very superior. 'You need to get up earlier!' said the Bedside Alarm. 'You don't eat properly, that's your problem!' shrieked the Kitchen Timer. 'You've got to get organised!' shouted the Office Clock. 'What do you expect with all this digital nonsense!' sneered the Silver Carriage.

Dennis felt sad and went to see his friend the Grandfather Clock. 'You're run down, laddie' said the Grandfather. 'I'll fix you an appointment with the Watch Mender'. The Watch Mender took one look at Dennis and said: 'Nothing wrong with you; you need a new battery, that's all!' Dennis was so relieved! He had his new battery fitted and immediately started ticking in time. The Owner was very pleased and never shook or tapped Dennis again. The Clocks were sorry they'd been so horrible and put on a special party to celebrate Dennis's new life!'

Tell the story using instruments. Choose some pupils to be The Clocks all ticking in time. Select one to be Dennis – always behind at first, then with his new battery …

Going on a school trip

School trip

Moderato

1. We're going on a school trip, excitement's in the air, we're going on an outing today. The coach is really crowded, there's not a seat to spare, our parents came to wave us on our way. We like clipboards and pens, doing research in a methodical way. We like finding things out learning it all by the end of the day.

2. We've listened to the teachers and answered all our names, we've pockets full of sweets we can munch. We're gazing out the window and playing silly games, can't wait until it's time to eat our lunch! Sitting on the back seat singing a song, waving at the drivers as we go. Sitting on the back seat jogging along proud to be the loudest in the class.

3. Our bags are simply bulging with waterproofs and drinks and suncream if the weather turns hot. We've magazines and cam'ras and yes the kitchen sink! You'd never guess just what a lot we've got!

repeat twice

The coach

1 Engines make an enormous variety of sounds. Children are quite naturally attuned to these variations: listen to any group of five year olds in the playground and you will hear many imitation engines as they zoom round Brands Hatch or loop the loop in a display of aerobatics. Talk to them about these sounds. When a vehicle goes faster, what happens to the sound of the engine? When it slows down? Who can imitate these sounds with their voices?

2 As well as the background sound of the engine, there are many other interesting percussion sounds on coaches. What rhythm might the windscreen wipers make? Indicators? Reversing alarm? With a small group of pupils, compose a short sound collage using voices and untuned percussion.

3 How could the sounds and music invented in activities 1 and 2 be modified to create a rhythmic accompaniment to 'School trip'?

The train

1 Trains sounds are wonderfully rhythmic. Chant 'quarter-to-two, quarter-to-two …' over and over with the class. Start slowly and build up to a medium pace. Gradually drop the vowels out until you have 'qu-t-t-t, qu-t-t-t …' Alternate between 'quarter-to-two' and 'qu-t-t-t'.

2 On a train you'll hear many rhythms at the same time. While one pupil or group keeps the 'quarter-to-two' rhythm going, experiment with other rhythms at the same time. Try 'chuka, chuka, chuka, chuka'. What about some irregular rhythms that appear for a few seconds and then disappear? Form three groups and build your train rhythms using vocal sounds.

3 Make the train go faster and slower. What other sounds can you add? How does the sound change going through a station, or in and out of a tunnel? What happens to 'quarter-to-two' when the train goes over some points? 'Quarter-to-two, quarter-to-two, quarter-to, quarter-to, quarter-to-two'.

4 Transfer the rhythms to appropriate instruments. Start with a group of three – one child on each part – and gradually add more children to each of the parts. Experiment. Which sounds give the best impression of a train? Why?

5 There are many wonderful pieces of music about trains. One of the more unusual ones that should be better known is *The Copenhagen Steam Railway Galop* by Danish composer Hans Christian Lumbye. Children love it. Listen also to 'Stimela' from the album of the same name, performed by South African jazz trumpeter Hugh Masekela.

6 Try and get a video of the classic 1936 *Night Mail*, a documentary on the London to Scotland postal special. Two of the greatest artists of the 20th century – poet W.H. Auden and composer Benjamin Britten – collaborated to make this short film.

Short ride in a fast machine

This is the name of a famous piece of music by American composer John Adams. Listen to a recording of the piece and discuss it with the children. How does the music give us the feeling of travelling at great speed? What's the vehicle like? Is it from the future? Who could create their own *Short ride in a fast machine*?

A ride in a charabanc!

What would school trips have been like a hundred years ago? In Edwardian times you may have travelled in a charabanc; a carriage with benches. To begin with these were horse-drawn. What would a charabanc have sounded like?

Which instruments could best give the impression of horses' hooves? How would the sound of the hooves change on different surfaces? What about when the horses go faster or slower, or come gradually to a stop? What would a horse-drawn charabanc sound like if it were in the next street, gradually coming nearer?

Contrast the sounds of the modern coach with those of the charabanc. Play the children's pieces side by side.

Postcards in sound

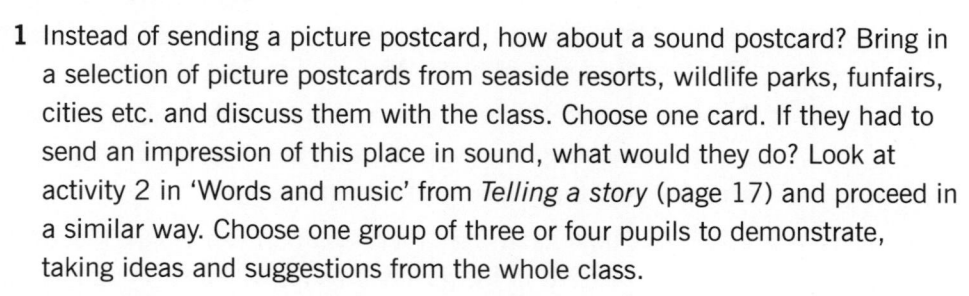

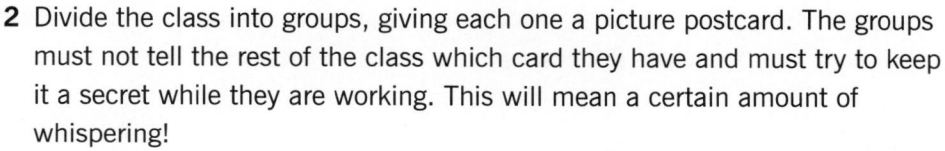

1 Instead of sending a picture postcard, how about a sound postcard? Bring in a selection of picture postcards from seaside resorts, wildlife parks, funfairs, cities etc. and discuss them with the class. Choose one card. If they had to send an impression of this place in sound, what would they do? Look at activity 2 in 'Words and music' from *Telling a story* (page 17) and proceed in a similar way. Choose one group of three or four pupils to demonstrate, taking ideas and suggestions from the whole class.

2 Divide the class into groups, giving each one a picture postcard. The groups must not tell the rest of the class which card they have and must try to keep it a secret while they are working. This will mean a certain amount of whispering!

3 When the pieces are ready to perform, take the postcards from the groups and display them. When each group has performed its piece, the rest of the class must guess which card it is representing. Tape the pieces and see if another class can tell which sound picture is which.

4 Link the sound postcards with the travelling pieces composed in 'The coach' and 'The train'.

Visiting museums and galleries

Sound pictures

1 Look again at 'Words and music' in *Telling a story* (page 17). Use people, animals, objects or events from pictures as your stimulus instead of words. Focus particularly on the movement of people and animals. How would the woman in the ball gown move? What about the cat? Could we invent some music to go with the movement?

2 Find two pictures or illustrations; one of an old castle and one of a witch. What was life like in the castle? How would the witch move? See if you can build up aural representations of the pictures.

3 Listen to two extracts from the orchestral version of *Pictures at an Exhibition*, Modest Mussorgsky – 'The Old Castle' and 'Baba Yaga' (the Russian witch). Discuss Mussorgsky's sound pictures. What do they have in common with the children's?

4 Perform the two childrens' pieces one after the other. Can they compose a short piece linking the two pictures, like someone walking from one to the other? Would they walk quickly or slowly?

5 Listen to 'Promenade' from *Pictures at an Exhibition*, Modest Mussorgsky. Are there any pictures in the gallery that you will be visiting that could be interpreted musically in this way? How could these activities be adapted to introduce the children to a museum artefact?

Sound collage

Take a piece of sugar paper and some small items that make interesting sounds. Try a piece of sandpaper, a piece of corrugated plastic or cardboard, a yoghurt pot, a small cardboard box and a piece of velvet. Stick them onto the paper. The pot and box go on upside down so that you can tap the bottom. The collage must sound and look good. Work with four or five groups and display the collages so that they can be played as well as looked at. Can you invent some musical patterns on them? Who could invent a sound sculpture?

Foreground/background

Find posters of famous paintings and talk to the children about what they see. Where relevant, draw their attention to the notion of foreground and background.

Take Leonardo di Vinci's *Mona Lisa*, possibly the most famous painting in the world. Talk about how the eye goes immediately to the enigmatic smile of the subject; any conscious awareness of the background comes much later, if at all. Does the same happen in music?

Do a little advance research and then ask them what they can tell you about the backings for three top ten recordings. Move into jazz, classical music and music from around the world, playing examples where instruments or voices are supported by a backing. Then play some recordings of unaccompanied performances. Try *Syrinx*, Claude Debussy; an unaccompanied spiritual; a classical guitar solo or 'Tom's Diner', Suzanne Vega.

The idea is not to provide answers but to encourage the children to think about what they see and hear; bringing the background to the fore (and vice versa) through the use of dynamics (volume).

Mixing it!

Just as paint can be mixed to produce a spectrum of colours, so sounds can be combined to create different tones and textures. With two groups of children, try some 'colour mixing' with instruments. Experiment with different combinations; what do bells sound like in combination with wood blocks? If you use more of one sound than the other, what happens to the combined sound? Ask the bell group to play very quietly while the wood blocks are loud and vice versa. Add as many new colours to your palette as you can. Keep mixing and experimenting.

Perceiving detail

Choose a painting that has plenty of action and detail. Try Rembrandt's famous *Night Watch*. Before you 'unveil' it, tell the children that you want them to jot down as many individual details as they can in one minute. Say that you want to see who can pick out the most. The details can be anything; dog, small girl, man in black hat, large drum. As soon as you can get them really looking, you can lead them to make more subtle observations. Use illustrations from books you are reading as well.

Now do the same with a piece of music; try a current pop song. The details could include instrumentation, lyrics, shape of the song, how it begins or how it ends. Write all the observations up on the board. Again, start to make more searching observations at this point. Adapt the materials to the ages of the pupils you're teaching.

Colour and black and white

What happens when you turn the colour button down on your television? Gradually the colour is drawn out of the image and you're left with a black and white picture. Then you can reverse the process and fill the image up with colour again.

Clap a simple rhythm with the class. Try 'knick knack paddy whack' repeated over and over again at a moderate tempo. Don't tell the children it's a nursery rhyme rhythm! Get it as sharp and precise as you can. Then ask the class how they could introduce colour into this rhythm pattern. They could play it on instruments. What colours do they want? How are they going to mix the sounds? Do they want the same instruments all the time? How else could they vary the colour? Could they add a melody? Harmony? Work with a group of five or six. Can they perform the black and white version alternately with the colour one? Can the colour button be turned slowly so that the colour is infused into the black and white version gradually? For a longer project, divide the whole class into groups.

Patterns and structures

These activities would be ideal as a preparation for a visit to a textile, costume or design museum, or to a gallery of contemporary art.

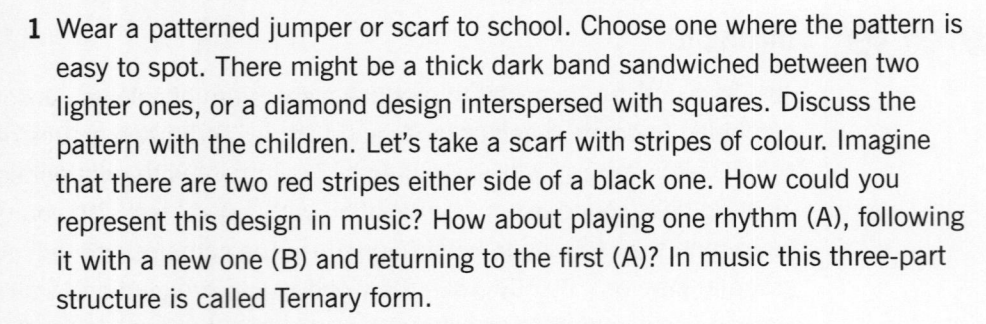

1 Wear a patterned jumper or scarf to school. Choose one where the pattern is easy to spot. There might be a thick dark band sandwiched between two lighter ones, or a diamond design interspersed with squares. Discuss the pattern with the children. Let's take a scarf with stripes of colour. Imagine that there are two red stripes either side of a black one. How could you represent this design in music? How about playing one rhythm (A), following it with a new one (B) and returning to the first (A)? In music this three-part structure is called Ternary form.

2 Clap a ternary form piece to the class. Try:
   A   Polly put the kettle on
   B   One for my master
   A   Polly put the kettle on

Clap them without any pause in between (**CD track 31**). Ask the class to join in. Can they make up their own ternary patterns working in small groups? What other patterns could they invent?

Mechanical museum

Invent a sound machine by putting several repeating rhythms together, both one after the other and simultaneously. Have fun choosing the most 'mechanical' instruments and sounds. What's the machine for? Include some machine-like movement and don't forget to use silence! Adapt this idea if you're going to a transport or a toy museum.

Listen to history

Where figures or events from history are referred to or represented, try to find some recordings of the music of that era. If the children are going to see Hans Holbein's *The Ambassadors*, listen to some Tudor music with them. What music was popular when Queen Victoria came to the throne? What do we know about the Ancient Greeks and music? Ask your top juniors to do some internet research.

The last day of term

School concert

1. Review the most successful and enjoyable music activities that you and your pupils have been involved in over the term. Are there any that the children could present at a school concert? Choose two or three possibilities and discuss them with the class.

2. What would need to be polished or adjusted in preparation for performance? Could anything be added to give it more appeal? Is it the right length? Would costumes be appropriate? Could any of the children's artwork form a backdrop? How much extra rehearsal is needed?

3. Plan a classroom performance of music that your pupils have enjoyed during the term. The concert could include songs and classroom compositions. You may have a recorder group and there will be children who learn other instruments who would like an opportunity to play in front of the class. Who would sing a solo?

4. Play some of the music you have created and performed. How should you plan the programme? Discuss ways that you can achieve a balanced and varied concert. Should there be a presenter?

Alternative endings

Review some of the pieces that the children have invented during the term. If you have taped any listen to them again, or see if you can reconstruct a particular favourite. If you created incidental music in activity 3 of 'Words and music' from *Telling a story* (page 17) – perform it again.

How did the piece end? Could the children provide a different ending? Could different instruments be used? What about the use of silence? *Crescendo* and *diminuendo*? Tempo? What effect does the new ending have on the whole piece?

Encore!

Explain that if an audience is particularly thrilled by a performance, the artist may give an encore. What do the children think would make an ideal encore? Should it be long and heavy, or short and light? Ask them to give reasons.

What songs do they think their favourite singers should sing as an encore? Have any of the children seen their concerts live or on video? What was the last song to be sung? Can they bring in a recording of this song?

Effective endings

Discuss the importance of a good ending in musical performance. As the last thing the audience will hear, it will be remembered …

Sing the endings of some of the songs they've sung and have some fun doing them badly! At the end of 'School trip' (page 39) sing 'Proud to be the loudest in the class' as quietly as you can, or shout the last line of the lullaby 'Hush-a-bye baby'.

Stress the importance of holding the silence for a split second at the end of a piece. Good conductors freeze and allow the music to hang in the atmosphere, particularly at the end of a quiet piece. Find a video of a great conductor doing this.

Going out with a bang! (Or a whimper …)

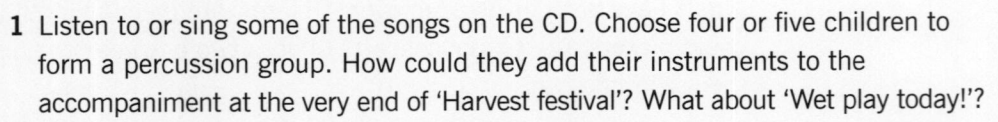

1 Listen to or sing some of the songs on the CD. Choose four or five children to form a percussion group. How could they add their instruments to the accompaniment at the very end of 'Harvest festival'? What about 'Wet play today!'?

2 Find recordings of loud, dramatic musical endings. Try Igor Stravinsky's ballet *The Rite of Spring*. What happens at the very end of the ballet?

Tidying up

Tidying up with music provides great opportunities for blackmail and bribery!

1 Agree to play a favourite recording, but only with the proviso that by the end of track 2 the cupboard/box/shelf/desk is completely tidy. If this is achieved, they can listen to a bonus track of their choice.

2 With the little ones, make up a 'Tidying-up song' and game. Try this, to the tune of 'Polly put the kettle on':

'Michael put the toys away,
Michael put the toys away,
Michael put the toys away,
Then please sit down.'

If there's a big tidying job to be done, sing 'Children put the toys away'. If you want something more general to sing as you tidy, try 'Children make the classroom neat'.

3 Watch the wonderful 'A spoonful of sugar' sequence from *Mary Poppins* and then tidy up.

Songs of farewell

There are many beautiful songs of farewell; look through a book of folk songs from anywhere in the world and you'll find some. There are also numerous pop and rock songs about parting and endings. Make a list from your own collection of CDs or ask the children to bring in examples. If you want a good laugh, try Peter Cooke and Dudley Moore's *Goodbye-ee*.

Auld Lang Syne

It's rare to find anyone who can sing all the words, tell you who wrote them and what they mean; yet this must be one of the most famous songs ever written. Ask some top juniors to do some research on the internet. Then sing the song together.

End game

Sing to 'la' the last line of a song the children have sung. Who can sing the first line? Once they've got the hang of it, try it with any melody: *The Pink Panther Theme*; *The National Anthem*; a nursery rhyme … but they must sing the first line, not just blurt out the name.

Biographies

Lin Marsh's experience with young singers, whether in the classroom or on the concert platform, is second to none. She has worked extensively in music education and has been an advisory teacher of music in Oxfordshire for twelve years. As well as directing Oxfordshire Youth Music Theatre, she has been a vocal coach and Musical Director for National Youth Music Theatre. Lin has travelled the country inspiring teacher, vocal groups and young singers with her dynamic workshops and lectures.

Richard Frostick's broad and extensive experience of teaching has encompassed all age-ranges and schools, including ten years in inner-city comprehensives. An LEA inspector for seven years, Richard now advises the BBC on music education matters and is a consultant adviser to schools and local education authorities. He has also collaborated with leading British orchestras on many education projects, and is in demand as an animateur and workshop leader both here and abroad. Richard founded and directs the Islington Music Centre.

Recommended resources from Faber Music

Junior Songscape and **Junior Songscape: Earth, Sea and Sky** Lin Marsh
Two invaluable collections of songs for Key stage 1 and 2 covering a range of musical styles, from music theatre, pop classics and rounds, to original pieces by Lin Marsh.

Sound Beginnings Richard Frostick
In simple terms, *Sound Beginnings* provides practical strategies for teaching children to perform, compose and appraise music of all kinds – with ideas for five-minutes activities to more extended classroom projects.

The show must go on! Lin Marsh and Wendy Cook
Whether teacher, performer, first-time director or experienced stage-hand, this practical guide is a starting point for a first venture into music theatre, or a source of new ideas if you are an old hand.

Kick-start your choir Mike Brewer
Presenting a treasure trove of ideas distilled from years of innovative work with singers of all ages, practical strategies are offered on almost every aspect of choral directorship.

RecorderWorld Pam Wedgwood
RecorderWorld is an exciting and creative way to learn the recorder. Incorporating key skills of musicianship and games galore, it is also the ultimate classroom resource.

Tam Lin Lin Marsh
Based on a Celtic folk legend, *Tam Lin* is a musical for key stage 2 and above, with ample scope for the addition of movement through which to illustrate the story.

A Minibeast Christmas Pam Wedgwood and Debbie Needle
Based on a Key stage 1 science topic, this musical is a variation on the traditional Christmas story, told from a rather unusual viewpoint.

The Christmas cobweb Pam Wedgwood and Debbie Needle
This is a charming and magical musical with memorable unison songs for Key stage 1.

Contents

Introduction 2
Tips on singing 3
Taking the register 4
Wet play 6
Teeth 9
Sirens and bells 12
Harvest festival 14
Telling a story 17
Sports day 19
In the dinner queue 22
Builders in school 26
Computers 29
Ceremonies and special occasions 32
There's a bee in the classroom! 34
Late for school 36
Going on a school trip 39
Visiting museums and galleries 42
The last day of term 45
Biographies 47
Recommended resources 47

Index of songs

Computer crazy 29
What shall we bring for the Harvest festival? 14
I can hear a bee! 34
Lunchtime rap 22
Late again 36
Please don't take a photograph! 9
School trip 39
Sport day samba 19
The building song 26
Wet play today! 6